THE STARTED COLT

Horsemanship as an Art

BRET DAVIS

PAGE PUBLISHING, INC.
Conneaut Lake, PA

First originally published by Page Publishing 2021

ISBN 978-1-6624-4225-4 (pbk)
ISBN 978-1-6624-4226-1 (digital)

Printed in the United States of America

This work, as with all my work, is dedicated to my wife. Nothing in life has ever been so pleasing to me than to get up every morning and go to work for her. And to my children: perhaps someday they may care to know what their dad thought about, and they can read this and possibly understand a little.

A Muse

"Don't try" was poet Charles Bukowski's secret for finding inspiration in his art, and with that muse, he wrote over forty-six books of short stories and poems, plus countless newspaper articles. Nothing forced can be beautiful. The very best we can do is create a place for beauty by setting a scenario for beautiful things to happen. Then we wait. It doesn't always happen on canvas or paper; it doesn't always happen with notes and sound. More often than not the masters throw away half-finished pieces, the evidence of a muse gone astray. The wastebaskets of poets, authors, painters, and composers are filled with bits of work that would have changed the world if only the muse could have been subdued long enough to be captured in ink. The halls of dance studios have witnessed feats of athletic ability and skill that could be executed but once or twice, but never mastered. Poets toy with a sentence until a word is found that can, in some small way, capture a piece of an idea, and that may be all that is done. A composer changes the structure of a symphony to fit in a note that manifests the emotion he is searching for, and a dancer tries again and again until the muscles learn the movement required. In the end, if the poet fails, he can throw the piece away, drink several whiskeys, and start again in the morning. The composer can toss an unfinished symphony, drink a few gin and tonics, and start again in the morning. A dancer can brush herself off, take two aspirins, and start again in the morning. A half-finished horse cannot be discarded so easily, and the lines drawn by the flawed hands of a horseman cannot be erased or covered up. They are part of the horse for the rest of its life. The brilliance of a fine finished horse shines so brightly the imperfections of the horseman are nothing more than shadows that scatter behind the light of the horse and, like shadows, make the light seem all the brighter. When horsemanship is practiced as an art, the horseman must simply put away his tools and wait for tomorrow when the muse and inspiration in himself or the horse is in threat of going astray. For centuries the masters of the art have run their hand across the sweating neck of a horse and said, "I have not yet broken anything in you that I cannot fix. I will be done for the day and try to teach you more tomorrow." Every day we build on the work we did the day before and strive to keep the action clean and the movement pure. Every evening we replay in our mind the day's events and catch the places where we as horsemen failed the horse. Every day we struggle. Every day we try to advance our horses and mitigate our mistakes in hopes of the day when the horse takes the work that no man can finish and finishes it himself.

A common phrase among horsemen is, "If you advance a horse by 1 percent every day, then in one hundred days the horse will be 100 percent advanced." The simplicity of the statement is definitive of the art, but it cannot be done. The greatest horseman in the world cannot advance a horse 1 percent a day for one hundred days in a row. The masters of the art of horsemanship advance a horse by fractions of a percent as often as the horse allows them. The very smallest degrees of advancement are gained and lost in every ride, to be averaged out at the end of the day. The men and women that have mastered the art have done so because they can read in the horse's movement and demeanor when the horse will allow advancement. The masters have sharply honed the practices of the art because they understand their muse, the horse.

MY STARTING

I used to think that it didn't matter who started a horse or what was done. I have managed to prove myself wrong and am very glad. It wakes me up at night, thinking of the things I did to horses because I didn't know any better. The crime cannot be mitigated by the reckless arrogance of youth. I think that a horse remembers his starting and remembers the things that happened in that time. I remember mine. I remember all the lessons that were shown to me over and over, and I remember when I finally learned how to learn.

I didn't choose this work; the work chose me. It's not that I grew up wanting to be something else and ended up making my living off a horse's back. It's that I didn't really intend to be anything in particular, and there was always a horse that needed riding. I didn't try.

I grew up in Southwestern Oregon, a place in the world that, for many people, the horse is a part of the culture, and I cannot remember a time that horses were not around. My friends and siblings rode, raced, swam, and spent most of our time on horses. At a very young age, people started asking me to put miles on their young horses and to put the first rides on colts. I was always amazed that people would pay me to ride a horse because it was something I was going to do anyway. Looking back on the skill level I had in those days, I am even more amazed. The me of today would not let the twelve-year-old me on a young horse. I didn't have sympathetic hands or good timing or even a plan for what to do, much less the knowledge of how to do it. At the time my only redeeming qualities with regard to a horse was that I was not afraid, and I bounced well. Everyone was always bragging about how well I bounced.

It seems odd to me that starting colts has somehow become work reserved for the young and the reckless, when it is so obviously work better suited for the aged and reserved. I can remember being asked what I was going to do when I got a little older. "You can't start colts forever, you know"—and I wonder now what makes people think that. I'm not sure why I can't start colts and train young horses my whole life. I am so much better at my work now than I was ten years ago and will be so much better ten years from now that I will be embarrassed of this book and my own artless and unworldly thinking. The way things have gone so far, by the time I am ninety, I ought to be able to think a horse into being trained without ever getting out of my wheelchair. Age and experience on a horseman is the patina of fine art that makes it worth so much. The young horseman catches and corners the horse and insists that the horse allow itself to be touched. The older horseman thinks of a way to get the horse to come up and asked to be touched. It may be that the patience and measured influence of the horseman can best be got by being bounced on the ground as a youngster.

In the valley that I grew up in, there were several old men that raised a few horses every year. Those men would have me put the first few rides on their colts. They mostly wouldn't let me put anything on the horse's head or wear spurs; I got a saddle and a rope around the horse's neck. For all intents, I was a test dummy. Some of those old men even called me that. I could tell that those men knew everything in the world I wanted to know about, things about life and love, horses, people, the phases of the moon—everything. The trouble was, they wouldn't talk to me. If I asked a question, they would ignore me and would only ever tell me what I was to do. At some point, it occurred to me that all these old men smoked and really only talked when they stopped to smoke. I think I was twelve when I started buying cigarettes and carrying them in my shirt pocket. Anytime I saw an old man (any old man, it didn't matter to me if I knew him or not), I would offer him a smoke and quiz him about the world. I was paid richly for my small offering. Those men would contemplate my question for a drag or two then wander off into their memory, forgetting for a moment that they were talking to a boy, and dictate a lifetime of experience to a young mind. When they reached the butt end of the cigarette, they would snap back into their aged bodies and look around with mourning at the reality they were in that was not the soft pastel of memory. Most would look at me and gruffly say, "What am I talking to you for? You are just a boy," but most would smile a little. I would like to find some old men like that again, but old men don't smoke anymore. I didn't always ask about horses, but the conversations always led to them. All examples of love and life and beauty and freedom, all courage and heroism, all strength and all faith were compared to a horse. Even things like shaving were compared to horses. "Shaving cream is like branding a horse. Time you think you got enough you have already done too much." Slowly I came to understand that there is more to a horse than four legs and a tail.

Ancora Imparo

I am still learning.

—Michelangelo, age 87

There are several world-class horse trainers in the valley I grew up in, and as I got older, I went to work for most all of them, always starting colts, and many of the colts went on to have big careers in the performance world. I am certain that the success of those early horses was due entirely to the talent of the horse and the trainer because I know they did not get the start they deserved from me. It saddens me now to think of it. At the time, I wasn't trying to learn the art; simply put, I preferred starting colts to any other work. So few are willing to start colts and ride young horses professional trainers are willing to put up with a lot of shenanigans from a young man that will get on one. I could come and go as I pleased and disappear for weeks at a time on rodeo adventures (also designed for young men that don't like to work), and I was always welcomed back with a smile and more colts to ride. Trainers liked me because by then I no longer bounced; all the bouncing had developed my riding to the point that I could ride about anything. I suppose that was what the old men that called me "test dummy" were aiming for. I was also well liked by trainers because I wouldn't fight a horse. It wasn't the benevolence in me that kept me from fighting with them but the fact that fighting with a horse is very hard work and rarely pans out. I have always been one for thriftiness in those regards and have never much cared for hard work. I did not realize that I was learning about horses, how they move think and act. I was gathering knowledge, but I didn't know what it was good for. If anyone had asked me why I did one thing or another or how to do something, I would have had a hard time answering because I was conditioned to watch a horse but not trained to think about one. I had all the information in my head about a horse, how one sees and how one moves, but I didn't use it. I sifted past horses for several years, riding on the blessings of youth, and never bothered to think about what made a horse react to me or me to the horse.

I think I was eighteen or maybe nineteen, and I took a job for the winter, trying out horses for a big horse buyer. I took the job offer on a whim and never thought twice about it, yet it is that job that changed the way I thought and made me a horseman.

The man I worked for had buyers working for him all over, and the horses would come in from all over the country. Double-decker cow trucks (back when that was legal) filled with all manners of horseflesh, all colors and shapes and breeds and ages. More horses than I had ever seen. They stepped off the truck, and I stepped on them, one at a time, to see what they were. I was back to being a test dummy, but I loved it. It was fast and exciting; and while I worked my tail off, it never seemed like work at all, just like one long, ongoing drama, punctuated by old studs trying to bite me and wild young-sters falling on me, kindhearted kid horses whose kids had grown up and majestic old souls who had made their last journey, and I would be the last to ever sit on their back. I was paid a fixed sum for each ride, so naturally, I swung a leg over every horse that walked off the truck because every horse was eight dollars to me. Thinking back, I cannot believe I risked my life so many times for eight dollars, and I am sad to think I profited off those old-timers that worked so loyally for so long. For eight bucks I made them carry a man one last time around the corral before they rested their old knees forever. I cry when I think about it.

Some of those horses would be ridden a little and resold as sad-dle horses; those that bucked hard went on to be rodeo broncs, and others served other purposes. The saddle horse candidates went in a pen full of wild kids off the rez that would ride double and triple bareback with only a piece of rope half hitched around the lower jaw. The horses didn't need to be very gentle because those kids had the horses outnumbered. I sort of wonder whatever happened to those kids. That pen of horses would get tortured by kids until they would stand for anything then get hauled off and sold as kid horses. A lot of those "kid horses" I saw a second and third time, and eventually, they went to the bronc pen. The horses that bucked hard went into a pen with feed bunks filled to the brim with alfalfa to be fed up and strong when they tried them as broncs. The horses that would fit neither bill went down a long ally, and I never saw them again. I was always pleased when one bucked hard because that was the best gate I could open for them. Some horses were kind and gentle, lacking only an education to make a saddle horse. Some were wild, some were scared, some had been educated in a way that they would never forget and were mean. Nearly every day I would recall the words of one of the old men of my childhood, "If you teach a horse a lesson in meanness, don't be surprised if he learns it." I got paid eight dollars a head for every horse I got on, and I got on a pile of them that winter. It was dangerous work, and I knew it, but I didn't care. The money was good for a kid that didn't know anything or want anything, and the danger in the work was pleasing to my reckless nature.

One evening I was cooking my supper and licking my wounds, and I was struck with a terrible thought. I knew the only reason I had the job was because I was more scared of being hungry than I was of any horse that stepped off the truck, but what if someday I wasn't? The idea terrified me, and worse, what if some other yahoo came along that was more scared of hunger than me? What if he was so scared of not eating he was willing to get on any horse around for six dollars? I thought about it for a long time and decided that it was inevitable that one of the two or both was bound to happen eventually. I decided that the only thing that stood between me and starvation was becoming so good with horses people would pay me to work them even if someone else would do it cheaper and be so knowledgeable about horses I didn't need to weigh my fear of hunger against my fear of a horse because I would be able to teach any horse. A flood gate opened in my mind that night, and all the things I'd been told and had seen started to have meaning and resonance to me. I devoted myself to sifting through the knowledge I had gathered and gleaned and figuring out what it all meant. Learning proved to be exponential, and everything I learned changed the things I thought I once knew and opened the doors to more learning and more. I learned how to learn, how to go forward and backward, side to side, and how to stop. Slowly I realized ways to refine the knowledge and boil it down to simple and correct facts that would always hold true. I am still learning.

From that time to now I have been blessed to work for and around some amazingly talented horsemen. I have been blessed to be married to a lady that also sees a horse as a canvas that can be painted to look like anything the heart desires. And I have been blessed to still feel like my life's work is a lark and a fun way to make a living because I never much cared to work.

THE ART OF HORSEMANSHIP

All good things come through grace, and grace can only
be attained by art, and art is got by hard work.

As much as I profess to being allergic to hard work, I seem to spend a lot of time doing it. I have yet to see anyone ever gain a thing by anything other than hard work. Luck is not real, and talent is overrated. I would happily trade a pound of any talent I may have for an ounce of work ethic. A horse cannot be trained by luck or talent or any sort of feeling. A horse is trained by work, and the human does more work than the horse.

For most all intents and purposes, anyone can sit on a horse if the horse will allow it and be carried around from place to place by the horse. There is no great feat in being carried by a horse. To ride a horse with specific intent with regard to space and time requires a set of skills. One must choose to hone the skills required to ride and train a horse; the choice is an expression of self, an expression of the way one wants to be and wants to be seen and, therefore, is an art. To be a horseman is to practice an art. It has been said by master horsemen that anything beautiful cannot be forced: a dancer, a painting, or a horse. The movement of a fine-finished horse, like a symphony, begins in the mind of the artist and is built piece by piece, note by note, footfall by footfall, until it is a thing of its own, no longer belonging to the horse or the horseman but to art and the practice of perfection. A horse that has been trained by art moves by art and seeks to create art himself.

There are many books that strive to teach a reader how to ride or train a horse. This is not one of them. This book strives to introduce the basic theories of the art of horsemanship, the tools of the horseman, and to introduce the horse itself. The art of horsemanship is a three-part series starting with this book, *The Started Colt*, where the process of starting a colt will be discussed. The next book, *The Next Three Years*, discusses the training of a horse from a started colt on through the refinement needed for finish. The final book, *The Finished Horse*, deals with the practices involved in finishing a horse as an art form.

Starting a horse is much like starting any other long-term project in the sense that the craftsman must know exactly what it is he wants the finished product to be and have a careful and precise method for doing his work. Otherwise, the craftsman will be left with a hundred little unfinished products that don't fit together. In the case of a horse, the horseman must know what he wants the finished horse to be like and what he must do to help the horse realize his potential. The horseman rides the colt with the finished horse in mind and, therefore, allows the horse to see what is expected.

So many riders get on a horse day after day without a clear plan of the expectations being held for the horse. A horse ridden in this manner can only advance through pure accident. A horseman works a horse with a clear and precise idea of what manner of advancement he is striving for and exactly how he is going to bring the advancement to fruition. In this manner, the horseman can advance the horse incrementally and with great efficiency. It is not fast, it is slow, but slowly is generally the fastest way to do things.

Learning to Learn

*Education is not the learning of facts but
the training of the mind to think*

—Albert Einstein

A started horse is a horse that is prepared to learn under saddle and rider. A started horse has not necessarily learned any maneuvers or exercises yet; he is simply prepared to start learning. Inevitably, the horse manages to learn a few things in the starting process; however, while starting a horse, the horseman should only be concerned that the horse is learning to learn. A started horse knows how to learn.

Go, Stop, Turn

Starting colts should be kept simple because horses are simple creatures that think simple thoughts. Horses like things to be easy and to make sense. They cannot grasp abstract ideas. They do not think linearly. A started horse can go, stop, and turn; that is all the knowledge he needs to learn. Go, stop, and turn are the basic foundation for everything else that the horse will ever do. Every maneuver of the finest-trained and most-athletic horses is a refined movement of going, stopping, or turning. Simple.

After the horse is started, training begins. All training is refinement of the gaits. In the beginning stages of training, a horse learns how to carry a rider with extension in the walk, trot, and lope, as well as backing up. That is *go*. The horse learns how to carry a rider in collection in three gaits, how to halt and half halt. That is *stop*. The horse learns how to change directions from all three gaits and reverse. That is *turn*. When a horse knows how to go, stop, and turn, he is started. When he knows how to go, stop, and turn in any direction from any speed, he is trained.

CONFIDENCE

When acts of grace no longer require effort
you have found confidence.

—Pedro Cruz

When preparing a horse to learn, the great concern of the horseman is the young horse's confidence. High confidence in a horse directly correlates to the speed in which the horse grasps and accepts ideas as well as the quality of the performance in the horse's maneuvers. A horseman fosters high confidence in a horse by being specific and consistent in his expectations of the horse. Horses desperately want to know what their role is in a relationship with a horseman and what they are expected to do to fulfill this role. A horseman that is specific and consistent in his expectations of a horse finds a horse to be willing, eager, and accepting of guidance in his work and in the performance of his role. Specificity comes from riding with intention, working a horse with a plan, a purpose, and a set expectation for the outcome.

So many riders get on a young horse with no plan or intention of what the ride will be like. They grope around in a darkness of thought, looking for the horse to do something "wrong" that they can "fix." A horseman has an ideal of what every ride from the first ride on should be like and therefore rides the horse with the intention of attaining that ideal. The horseman plans the ride and the lesson; the mere rider sits on the horse and lets the horse (that at this point knows nothing about how to be ridden) make all the decisions. This practice of riding a horse without a specific plan makes no sense. The horse doesn't know what is supposed to happen. The horse is counting on the human to dictate and direct what is supposed to happen. I cannot overstate this. Never in my life have I said, "Well, I don't know what to do next. Let's just see what happens," and had the result be positive. I have learned a lot by going off half-cocked, but it was always to the horse's detriment and made more work for me later on.

I would like to add here that under the ideals with which I was educated about horses, there was a major difference between a rider and a horseman/trainer. I know some incredible riders that cannot teach a horse. The days I spend as a "test dummy" for the old men of my youth, I was a rider, but it was not until I started to develop some thought about the hows and whys of riding did I start to become a horseman. To this day I remind myself to be the pilot, not the passenger.

TOOLS

*The tool does not make the craftsman, but he
cannot build anything without them.*

—Martin Gutierrez

The first and most important tool a horseman can have is an understanding of the horse's body. This is also the most important tool he can give to a horse to learn with. An un-started and untrained horse has very little consciousness of his own body and what it is doing. The horseman must have this knowledge because if neither party knows what the horse's body is doing or is capable of doing, the project is failed before it ever starts. The horseman sees the horse's body as five independent systems. The five systems work in unison by nature but must be able to work independently for the horse to realize his full potential. This is true of any athlete.

The Five Parts of a Horse's Body

*Do you have any idea what your hands are
doing while you're trying to stay on?*

—Bob Nelson

There are five parts, or separate systems, to a horse's body; the five parts work in unison, but through training, the horse learns to use all five systems independently. The independent movement of a horse's body is the basis of a trained horse and is dependent on the independent movement of the rider's body. When starting a horse, and later when training and finishing a horse, the horseman is aided by the knowledge of the five parts of the horse's body and how they work. In order to orchestrate the independent movement of the separate systems, there is a necessity for the horseman to understand how the systems work together.

The five parts of the horse's body are head, neck, shoulders, barrel, and hip. Each of the five major systems is made up of multiple smaller systems that make up the system as a whole.

Head

The head consists of the upper and lower jaw and the poll. The "poll" is the atlas and axis of the horse's spinal column and forms the joint that connects the spine to the skull. This joint is specialized to allow greater range of motion than the rest of the vertebra and is responsible for the nodding and rotational movement of the head.

This joint allows for flexion of forty-eight degrees vertically and seventeen degrees horizontally before any flexion from the rest of the neck is required. Any increase in flexion or rotation from the neck that exceeds the capabilities of the poll starts with and is generally exclusive to the seventh and fifth vertebra. This is not a hard and fast rule but a rule of thumb. The axis is the longest vertebra in the horse's spine and houses the connection of the brain stem and the spinal cord. The horse is unique to other mammals in that there is a gap between the axis (C1) and the second cervical vertebra of the neck; in this gap the spinal cord is unhoused by the protective bone of the vertebra. This gap allows "poll pressure" when riding the horse. Poll pressure is applied when leading a horse or when engaging any bit or hackamore. This poll pressure is literally applying pressure to the spinal cord, inducing the horse to move away from or give to the poll.

The jaw of the horse is jointed to allow a "slip plate" action that enables the lower jaw of the horse to slip forward slightly when the poll is flexed vertically. If the horse's teeth are not floated properly, the sharp edges will catch when the jaw slips, and the horse will not properly frame at the poll. The upper and lower jaw also slip when a horse turns its head either left or right. Again, if the teeth are not properly floated, the horse will not be able to slip the jaw and will not be able to remain flexed at the poll when turning the head left or right. The horse will bypass the issue of the jaw not slipping by gaping the mouth through maneuvers or elevating the head. Proper flexion of the jaw and poll facilitate lateral and vertical flexion through the whole body. A horse that is rigid in the jaw or poll, either laterally or vertically, will be rigid in the rest of the body, and rigidity in other body systems can lead to a rigid jaw and poll.

Neck

The neck is made up of the seven cervical vertebrae (atlas included) and runs from the poll to the withers. In general terms, an ideal horse flexes the neck at C7, the shortest, widest, and last vertebra of the neck, and at C5. A horse uses the neck both as a lever (vertical elevation) that has a fulcrum at the withers (C7) and as a pendulum (horizontal flexion) that articulates at the withers or the joining of cervical and thoracic vertebrae to balance the weight of the horse's body in movement. In other words, the horse will use the strength of the neck as a lever to brace against the weight of the body to manipulate movement and retain balance in motion. The horse will also use the weight of the head (approximately 10 percent of the body weight) on the end of the neck to do the same. In this way, the untrained horse will raise or lower the head while in motion to brace against and balance the body or swing the head left or right to manipulate the kinetic energy and balance the body while in motion. In an untrained state, the horse will bend slightly at the neck (C5) opposite the direction of travel to offset the weight of the body in motion. The horse does this because it carries the majority of the body's weight on the front quarters. When in motion, the horse can leverage and swing the weight of the head on the neck to keep the body balanced. Collection is the activity of shifting the horse's center of balance and the majority of weight off the front quarters and onto the hindquarters. The balancing action of the horse's neck is one of the primary tools in this activity along with the hind legs. The freedom of movement in the neck, both laterally and vertically, liberate the shoulders and limbs to move with rhythm and cadence. In simple terms, it is entirely possible to overflex the neck and make collection nearly impossible. A high degree of flexion in the neck should be reserved for the finishing process when a horse is physically and mentally mature. All too often young horses are induced to hyperflex the neck at a young age. The young horse needs the strength of his neck to balance his body with the added weight of a rider. I remind myself that I have several years to refine the neck after the horse has learned to go, stop, and turn. Saddle fit is also an important consideration when considering the neck because an ill-fitting saddle can impede the way a horse uses the neck at the withers, where the cervical vertebrae join the thoracic vertebrae.

Shoulders

The shoulder blades of the horse partially house the junction of the cervical and thoracic vertebrae. This particular junction is referred to as the horse's withers. The neck, shoulders, and barrel of the horse tie in at the wither; this intersection is considered by many horsemen to be paramount to the structural integrity of the horse. There are five vertebrae in the withers between the shoulder blades. The horse has no collarbone; therefore, the barrel or torso is attached to the shoulders by muscles, tendons, and ligaments. This part of the body is incredibly strong yet extremely fragile by virtue of the amount of force the muscles can produce. The untrained horse carries the majority of weight on the shoulders and for limbs using the barrel (back and torso) and hips like a rudder to steer the body. The body moves counter or opposite to the balance of the neck and is directly affected by the direction and elevation of the head and neck. The horse in his untrained state moves crooked. However, the trained horse has shifted the majority of weight from the semi-fragile shoulders and for limbs to the more-stable back and hind legs and is therefore liberated in the shoulders to use the powerful muscles that bind the horse at the shoulder to move laterally and vertically with speed and precision. The power in the muscles of the shoulder combined with the lack of a collarbone for structural soundness is the predominant reason for the high frequency in soreness and injury to the shoulders. The horse literally tears itself up by virtue of its own strength. A large part of the training process is aimed at mitigating this tendency. The trained horse has shifted the majority of the body weight to the hind limbs and therefore has less tendencies toward injuries in other parts of the body. When starting a horse, a horseman begins to develop collection from the beginning by engaging a horse in a manner that will cause the horse to shift its weight and liberate the shoulders; a simple example would be turning a horse into a fence. When the horse turns into a fence rather than turning the horse into the corral, he must shift his weight back onto the hind feet in order to make room for himself to make the turn. If allowed to turn into the pen and away from the fence, the horse is able to make the turn on his front end without shifting his weight or liberating the shoulders.

The horseman can also use a horse's inclination to carry weight on the front end to keep the horse out of trouble; with relative ease, a knowledgeable horseman can load a horse's weight on the shoulders and four limbs and effectively retard all movement. This retardation of movement can be a handy tool on a young horse that is scared or mad but unfortunately has become the cornerstone of many modern training styles.

Barrel

The barrel of the horse consists of the eighteen thoracic vertebrae and each corresponding rib and the six lumbar vertebra of the loin that join the back and the hindquarter. (Some breeds, most commonly Arabs, have five lumbar vertebrae while others sometimes have seven.) There is a correlation between the length of the lumbar vertebra and the strength of the horse's back. Commonly, the horse with longer lumbar vertebra has a stronger back. The longissimus dorsi, while originating in the fourth cervical vertebra of the horse's neck, runs the length of the horse's back and ties in at the sacrum or croup. This muscle contracts the spine and is the main muscle of the back used for collecting and athleticizing the horse. It is the longest and singularly strongest muscle in the body of the horse. It is also the muscle that carries the majority of the rider's weight when on the horse. The barrel also consists of the abdominal muscles and sternum that aid in the support of the weight of the horse's internal organs as well as the weight of the rider. The barrel of the horse is considered rigid, as a horse has a rigid spinal column. There is very little flexion to be had laterally in the horse's body, and the majority of lateral flexion comes from the strength and elasticity of the abdominal muscles. This underline of a horse is actually very weak in comparison to the rest of the horse's muscle structure and is supported during high performance by the other systems. While the barrel is relatively rigid, it is imperative that the horse be as flexible as possible in the barrel to perform at maneuvers. The flexion of the barrel is dependent on the liberation of the shoulders from the horse's weight. Only when the hindquarters are engaged, producing the majority of impulsion in the horse's action, can the barrel and back lift to shift the weight and balance of the horse's body onto the hindquarters, thus liberating the shoulders and allowing for maximum flexibility in the barrel.

The longissimus dorsi originates at the fourth cervical vertebra of the neck. When a horse is severely "hollowed out," a term that indicates the opposite of collection, this muscle will bulge at its origin in the neck. The bulging is due to muscle atrophy caused by the horse constantly "hollowing" the back and neck. In my experience, with an un-started colt, this atrophy is almost always due to eating out of an overhead feeder of some kind. A horse is built to brows with its head below the level of the knee; this action flexes and stretches the muscle. Whenever I see this bulge in the neck, I know I am in for a lot of hard work because it is very, very difficult to gain any sort of impulsion and collection until this muscle gains fitness. Rehabilitating this muscle is very difficult. A few times over the years I have seen horses with this bulge due to training methods. Generally speaking, the "trainer" does a lot of exercises that counter flex the horse with its head elevated rather than counter flexing with the head down and neck flexed. Anytime I have questioned the exercise, I have been told that it is an effort to "free up" the horse's shoulders. Sadly, the exercise does the opposite. It is very easy for an uneducated rider to abuse a horse without knowing it.

Hindquarters

The hindquarters of the horse start at the sacrum. This is where the lumbar portion of the horse's vertebral column ties into the anchorlike structure of the sacrum. The sacrum is the fusion of between four and six, but usually five, of the horse's vertebra. The sacrum is considered the end of the horse's back; although the fifteen to twenty-one caudal vertebrae of the tail are indeed part of the spine and, to a small degree, will aid in the horse's balance. Of course, the tail of the horse is a necessity to the animal for many other reasons, from fly control to expression. For the sake of this particular discussion, the tail is nonessential. The sacrum articulates with the horse's two hip bones, the lumbar portion of the vertebral column and the tail. Like the withers where the back, shoulders, and neck junction, the sacrum area at the croup where the tail, hips, and back tie in is a very important consideration of the horse's conformation. The predominant factor of the horse's hindquarter is the hip, the driving force and motor of the finished horse. From first contact on through the finish training, the horseman strives to engage the horse's hips. The quest for collection begins with the movement of the horse, starting from the hind leg and progressing through training forward through the horse's body. Stride in the hind leg comes from articulation in the hip. The fitness of the muscles greatly increases the articulation of the hip and aid immensely in the carriage of weight on a collected horse. The abdominal muscles of the barrel also tie into the hindquarter at the flank; the fitness of the abdominal muscles also increase the articulation of the hip.

All training is refinement of the gaits. Refinement of the gaits starts with collection (the shift of a horse's center of balance from front quarters to hind); collection starts with the movement of the hind leg that engages the hip, allowing the back and barrel to lift. This combined action liberates the shoulders of the horse from the weight of the horse, allowing free movement and balance from a strong neck that can only be had when a horse has a loose poll and jaw. All five parts of the horse's body must work independently in order to work together.

Horsemen have been in a debate for centuries at least and probably around the campfires of ancient warring states and nomadic tribes for millennia. Under starlit sky, with the concerto of vast herds grazing across an endless plain in their ears, horsemen of long-forgotten traditions have debated the finer qualities to look for in a horse, and the tradition remains alive in barns around the globe as well as silver and porcelain laid tables where the fine horses of today are discussed. Which of the five parts of a horse's body is most important? Each camp has its points. The truth is, none of the five parts/systems can operate properly without the others nor can any one of the five operate properly if the multiple systems within each do not operate properly. The horse is not started or trained by beginning with one of the five parts, working through three more and ending with a fifth. Each of the five parts must be able to be isolated and worked independently to train the horse. Before any one part can be isolated, the horse must learn how to work the five parts together; this is the starting of a colt. When the horse can be held straight by the rider and moved forward and backward, side to side, go, stop, turn, with all five parts working in unison, the horse is started and prepared to be trained with independent movement of any or all parts of the body.

Around the globe, both riders and horsemen have catchphrases that they use about horses. One horseman may talk about "feel" while another notes a horse's "soft eye" or "cow pony ears" or "bridle horse neck." There are negative catchphrases as well: "pig-eyed" or "canoe-headed." I often hear about a horse's "grit" or "try" or "heart." I'll take good conformation over any of the positive catchphrases and in spite of any of the negative. Give me good conformation, and I will make the rest.

Five Parts of the Rider's Body

The five systems of the rider's body correlate directly with the five systems of the horse's body. Like the horse, the five systems of the rider's body are the head, neck, shoulders, barrel, and hips. Also like the horse, the five systems of the rider's body are made up of multiple smaller but no less important systems. Like the trained horse, the rider's body must be able to work in perfect unison as well as work with complete independence. At no point in the horse's training is the rider's body control more important than when starting the young horse. During the starting process, the horse is learning to carry its own body straight, controlled and in union; therefore, the horseman that starts the young horse must be in complete control of his or her own body and must be a first-class rider in order to offer the horse the opportunity to find balance. The horse cannot find balance in its body if it is constantly being thrown off balance by the rider. The horse can only find balance by driving itself into the balance of the horseman and synchronizing its timing with the timing of the horseman. The horseman is not born with this rare ability of body control and perfect consciousness of independence. While some people are blessed with a natural sense of balance and timing, all riders must develop balance and body control in order to become a horseman that can start and train a young horse. Like the dancer, the musician, and the horse itself, the horseman must practice in order to make art.

The Head

Like the horse, the horseman's head consists of the poll and jaw. The atlas and axis of the human body functions in a similar manner to the same joint of the horse's body, and our own head carriage has a direct effect on our balance as well as the balance and carriage of the horse. The horseman strives to ride straight at all times, meaning, if an imaginary line were drawn from the horseman's head to the heel, it would be a perfectly straight line; and if the horse was suddenly erased from under the horseman, he would find himself standing flat-footed, knees slightly bent, back and shoulders straight, and head up. Anytime the rider deviates from this position, the horse is compelled to adjust his own balance. Riding straight is imperative when starting a colt. The rider's body works like a lever on the horse, and the young horse can only balance if the rider is balanced. When the rider does not carry his head straight, he leverages forty pounds of pressure on the horse's shoulders for every inch off of center. The jaw of the rider is also important. In order to make a horse ride with a loose jaw, the rider must also have a loose jaw. Every time a rider clenches the jaw, the action causes the muscles in the shoulders, back, and abdomen to tighten. This action causes the horse to tighten in the shoulders, back, and abdomen, as well as defeating the loose balanced action that is sought.

The Neck

Like the horse, humans adjust their balance with the neck. Humans tend to carry their head and neck slightly off-center, flexing into the direction of travel. This tendency causes the front and hind limb of the horse on the inside of the direction of travel to slow slightly and the two limbs on the outside to speed up. Anytime a young horse finds himself out of balance, his first reaction is fear. The horse does not fear the situation; the horse fears the feeling of vulnerability that being out of balance causes. Being afraid, the horse will either try to speed up to find balance or contort the body to find balance. The only thing an untrained horse can do to find balance is adjust the speed of travel and bend the body. When the young horse speeds up and starts bending its body in a search for balance, we call it bucking. By remaining balanced, the rider will never scare the horse into bucking. At the time of writing this, I have put the first ten rides on forty-seven colts in the last sixty days; not one of them has bucked because I have not allowed one to lose balance. I don't bring this up to blow my own horn, only to point out that an experienced and professional colt starter should rarely, if ever need to, ride a bucking horse, provided that the young horse is raw and has not already been tried at by others. As horseman, if we are able to control our own bodies, movement, and balance, then controlling the body, movement, and balance of a young horse should be relatively simple. Unfortunately, as far as I know, there is no particular exercise program or regiment to learn this level of personal control. The only way I know of is getting on and riding lots of horses with a particular drive and consciousness as well as a knowledgeable teacher. I had a lot of wonderful horsemen and women to learn from, but my greatest teacher was bruises and broken bones. In my opinion, the latter is the best teacher, but I still wish I had paid more attention to the former.

The Shoulders

The shoulders of a human pull on the abdomen and back. Shoulders thrust forward pull on the rider's back, and shoulders thrust back pull on the rider's abdomen. Shoulders that are slumped or forward tend to push our weight down through our barrel, centering the weight in the space between our pelvic bones. This tends to cause the horse to hollow its back rather than round it. Loose, open shoulders flex the muscles of the abdomen that then liberate free flexion in the hips of the rider, inviting impulsion from the horse as well as a strong round back. The combination of the rigid abdomen and liberated hips in the rider creates a space for collection or the shifting of the horse's weight and center of balance off the shoulders and four limbs back onto the hind legs of the horse. A rider's shoulders dictate the expression of the horse's movement. A rider that slumps his shoulders creates a hollow horse, and a rider that has tight shoulders shortens the stride in the horse. A rider with loose, open shoulders creates a horse with a high, free-swinging back and an impulsive stride.

The Barrel

The human back tends to be much stronger than the abdomen, and riders tend to use the strength of the back to leverage their weight against their own hips and the horse's back to stay on the horse by force rather than balance. Over the course of a lifetime of riding, this posture will break a rider down and will sore the backs of many horses. The center of balance for a human is located in the abdomen, and fitness in these muscles greatly increases balance. A balanced rider is able to let the horse move under him and to stay out of the horse's way. This is particularly important when riding young horses. A rider that uses his back to leverage his weight against the horse to stay on will create a horse that does not want to move because movement is uncomfortable for the horse. Riding in this manner will also create a horse that must be handled in, and through, every movement because the horse is never liberated in its own movement enough to find a fast and efficient way of executing a maneuver. Like the horse, the rider has a limited level of flexion in the barrel compared to the rest of the body. Also like the horse, a rider with fitness in this part of the body will be able to maximize the limited amount of flexion and, in so doing, will help the horse maximize the flexible capabilities of the barrel. Due to the comparative strength of the human back, it is very easy for a rider to overlook this important part of the body. The chest and ribcage of the rider also play an important role in the movement of the horse. The pectoral region of the rider's body should be the most forward part of the body (besides the hands). This posture not only allows the rider to breathe better (therefore think better) but also creates freedom of movement in the lower back of the rider. A loose or free lower back liberates the hips of the rider. Once in a while I step onto a young horse and feel myself riding tight. As soon as I notice, I start to sing out loud. Singing opens my shoulders and ribcage as well as increasing my oxygen intake. This action frees my lower back and hips. Almost immediately I will feel my horse relax under me, and I promise, it is not because he enjoys the music.

The Hips

The rider's seat is the center for communication between horseman and horse. There is no other aid that can communicate as quickly and as efficiently as the seat. With the horse, all balanced movement must start with the hind leg and hips; and with the rider, all communication of balanced movement must start with the leg and hip. A rider that keeps the upper body balanced and loose over the hips will soon develop a horse the remains balanced and loose under the hips. Keeping the hips straight is very important. Many riders tend to want to shift or drop their hips into the direction of movement. This can only slow the inside hind leg of the horse, causing the horse to drop a shoulder into the turn. Other riders tend to shift the hips to the outside of the turn, causing the outside hind leg of the horse to step out rather than under the barrel. This movement hollows the horse and certainly ruins the integrity of a maneuver but with a young horse will often create fear in the horse because of the loss of balance. Some riders tend to drive the hips forward into the horse's action and impede the horse's ability to lift the shoulders and back. A horseman strives to keep the hips straight but loose and capable of articulation in an effort to aid the horse with directional control from the legs and feet. In the last twenty years, I have seen countless riders and some very popular schools of method that compel the rider to move the horse off balance or keep the horse off balance with the use of the rider's body in an effort to create a "quiet" and "confident" horse. The truth is, much of this type of methodology simply retards the horse's movement to the point that it can be ridden rather than teaching the horse to carry a rider. These types of practices are detrimental to the horse both physically and mentally.

THE HORSE'S EYE

I try to avoid comparing horses and humans at all cost because, for the most part, the comparison is apples to anvils. However, in the discussion of the horse eye, I find it necessary to compare the horse eyes to the human eye in an effort to clearly show what and how a horse sees.

The horse has the largest eye of all mammals in comparison to body size. In fact, other than the whale, the horse has the largest eye of all mammals. Over the centuries, poets and bards have sung of the beauty and majesty that lays within the flaming orb of perpetual depth that is the horse's eye, and many a youngster has fallen in love with the romance and mystery that can only be seen when one gazes into those pools of liquid fury and grace. When practicing the art of horsemanship, it is important for us as horsemen to concern ourselves with more than the beauty of the horse's eye and focus more on the function and capabilities of the eye. By understanding how the eye works, we can understand what the horse sees and come to a better understanding of how he acts and why.

With that said, let us, as horseman, never cease to be horse lovers that, like children, lose our wits and allow ourselves to be swallowed whole by the strange amber luminescence and swirling tide of unspoken emotion that can be seen only in the eye of a lover or a horse.

The eye of the horse is similar in design to the eye of most mammals in regard to structure and function. The horse eye differs from the eye of most other mammals because of its placement on the head. The retina of the eye is the mechanism that takes in light and processes the light as sight that is sent to the brain. Within the retina there are rods and cones. The horse has a twenty-to-one rod and cone ratio versus a two-to-one ratio in humans; the eye of the horse takes in ten times more light than the eye of a human. For obvious reasons, a horse can see better on an overcast day than a bright, sunny day and better overall in low-light situations. In a horse's eye the retina takes up two-thirds of the eye, so the horse is able to collect an immense amount of light. Horses are not color blind. They see in dichromatic vision, meaning, they see two of the three basic wavelengths of color that we humans see. In fact, there are a lot of wavelengths of light that humans cannot see. Most humans see three, and some birds see four. Some species of shrimp see many more. The existential backlash of this idea is incredible. One-third of the horse's eye is made up of the optic disk, which receives no light but is responsible for the communication between the eye and the brain via millions of afferent nerve fibers. The optic disk is also the point for the major blood vessels that supply the retina. Since this optic disk takes in no light, the horse has a blind spot in the center of the eye. Form to function the eye of the horse works in a very similar way to the human eye. The major difference in the two is that the horse's eye takes in much more light than ours, and the blind spot from the optic disk is larger in the horse. Also, humans have full binocular vision, and horses only have partial binocular vision. Because of the full binocular vision that humans enjoy, our brains are able to recreate what we see and fill in the tiny blind spot with what the brain reckons should be there. As a result, we humans do not notice the blind spot that the optic disk creates. Horses, on the other hand, are fully aware of their blind spot.

A horse's visual capacity is really incredible and somewhat different than the other monocular mammals because of the set of the eye and the set of the ear. The horse can see 350 degrees around with his peripheral monocular vision. This capacity is horizontal and can see seventy-eight to eighty degrees vertically, almost all the way around and from the ground, almost straight up. It is really incredible to think that the horse can see all four of its own feet and nearly directly above itself. There is also a blind spot directly in front of the horse at about four to six feet caused by the optic disk and directly behind the horse to a distance of about four feet. Of the 350 degrees in the horse's field of vision, only a 65-degree field can be seen with binocular vision (both eyes focused at the same point) while the monocular field of vision (both eyes seeing a separate picture) is 285 degrees. The total range of vision for a human is about 170 degrees.

The horizontal plane of binocular vision is triangular in shape and directly in front of the horse's face. Because of the horse's muzzle, the horse has a smaller field of depth perception than a human. To determine depth, a horse must raise or lower the head, increasing binocular range, with the head raised and focusing on closer objects with a lower head. The accuracy of the binocular focus would compare to 20/33 vision in a human. Small details that can be seen by a human at sixty meters can be seen by a horse with the same accuracy at twenty meters. At a distance of six feet, a horse can discern a difference in depth of about nine centimeters compared to a human that can discern a difference of just a few millimeters or the width of a few sheets of paper at the same distance. How do we know all this? We asked horses.

A horse has a "visual streak," a perpendicular line running across its field of vision. In this streak the horse's sight is best. There are 6,100 ganglion cell/mm2 in the visual streak compared to 200 cells/mm2 in the rest of the eye. A ganglion cell is a type of neuron located on the surface of the retina. They receive visual information from photoreceptors. Ganglion cells collectively transmit image-forming and nonimage-forming visual information from the retina to regions of the brain. The "visual streak" of a horse's vision collects more visual information to send to the brain than other parts of the eye. A horse's eye is more sensitive to motion than to depth, and the majority of motion in the wide field of vision is picked up in the peripheral vision outside of the visual streak. When the horse's eye catches motion in the less-acute visual field, the horse is inclined to move away first and try to focus on the motion with his more-acute "visual streak" from a safe distance. Because of the way a horse sees, he is hardwired to spook at movement in his field of vision and fly from it. This is part of why round pens work so well because the horseman stays within the "visual streak" at all times when on the ground.

A horse sees movement with monocular vision then turns the head to focus on the movement with binocular vision. A horse cannot use both binocular and monocular vision at the same time, so when the horse switches, the focus jumps and is distorted for a moment. The binocular vision is directed down the muzzle, not straight in front of them, so a horse must raise the head and look down the muzzle to focus and find depth with binocular vision. A horse working on the bit can only see the ground directly in front of him and depends on the rider to direct him around obstacles; a horse working behind the bit can only see its own front legs.

Studies of the equine eye show that horses are able to negotiate in light levels that are so low humans find sight impossible. This is to say that a horse can see in the dark because of the size, shape, and construction of his eye; he absorbs more light than we do. However, for the same reasons, the horse is not able to adjust to changes in light as fast as we can. It takes several moments for a horse's eye to adjust from high light levels to low light levels and vice versa. On the contrary, our own eye adjusts from high to low light very quickly and with extreme accuracy. Often horses shy from shadows or balk, going back and forth from levels of high light to levels of low light. When a horse steps out of a barn into the full light of day, he tends to pause and stare blankly. This is because he cannot see and is waiting for his eyes to adjust. If the handler leading the horse pulls on him, or the rider urges him forward before his eyes have adjusted, the horse plants his feet and refuses; many a fight has started this way. The horse cannot see and, of course, loses confidence in the situation, and the inconsiderate human adds force. In the resulting argument, the horse goes in and out of the high and low light, further confusing his vision. Regardless of how the situation works out, the end result is a horse that has less confidence than when he started. This goes for trailer loading and riding in and out of shaded areas as well. It takes a long time for a horse to develop the confidence to go blindly, in the literal sense, wherever he is asked.

About one-third of domestic horses are nearsighted; however, very few are farsighted. Nondomestic horses after about the sixth generation of living feral tend to be farsighted, and few are near-sighted. This is due to the necessities in the nature of being feral or domestic. I have heard people talk about working with feral horses and mention that the horse has less confidence around barns and other man-made objects than when in the open. People always seem to imply that the horse is distrustful of man-made objects because it is naturally distrustful of man. I tend to think that, in actuality, the horse becomes a little nervous around man-made objects because humans build structures in a manner that is confusing to the far-sighted feral horse. This is only a theory, and I shall ask the next feral horse I come across.

The ability to change focus accurately between far-off objects and objects that are near is called "sight accommodation." Horses have very poor sight accommodation, especially when compared to humans who have excellent accommodation in comparison to other mammals. Horses make up for the lack of sight accommodation by moving their head, holding it lower or higher, and changing the angle to suit the field of vision. Again, it is common for a rider to become frustrated with a horse that is carrying the head either too high or too low or cocking the head to one side or another in an effort to find focus on the object or obstacle in front of them. A very confident and very trained horse will follow the command of the rider with faith that he is being ridden into something safe; however, a young horse with few rides often must see for himself before he is willing to proceed through or over or into something he cannot focus on. Even some highly trained jumping horses will tilt their head slightly before jumping in an effort to find focus on the obstacle and depth of the jump. I think this is frowned upon in show jumping, but to me, that is actually pretty cool.

The horse's vision works on a horizontal plane. While they can see nearly 360 degrees around them with only a few degrees of obstructed vision, the focus of the eye is a thin strip in the center of the field of vision. Any vision below or above this focal strip is blurred. By contrast, nearly everything that falls into the human field of vision is seen with the same focus. To put it plainly, your horse is not an idiot; he really does see spooks and floating goblins all around him, and if he is not able or allowed to move his head to draw the object into his line of focus, the spook remains spooky. Liken this to seeing a wisp of movement out of the corner of your eye on the boundary of your field of vision. It gives you a start, but you turn your head and see it was a leaf falling or a squirrel squireling. If you were unable to turn your head and find the spook, you would panic. A horse sees with less focus than a human; however, he makes up for it with an incredibly broad field of vision and an extreme sensitivity to detecting movement.

A horse can see about six inches directly in front of his face and is then blinded by his own muzzle and the optic disk to a distance of four to six feet. Humans also can always see their own nose; however, our brain has developed to completely ignore the obstruction. Our brain reconstructs what we see, so the nose is left out while a horse always has something obstructing his vision. Imagine going through life with something being held in front of your face. You can see past it, over it, and below it, but you cannot see directly in front of you. Nature has given the horse sensitive whiskers on his muzzle to make up for this. When one approaches from directly in front of a horse, he can see the approaching person clearly and in detail at a distance; however, as one comes nearer, the details become blurry to the horse's vision in all parts that are not in the horizontal visual streak. At a distance of six feet, the horse can only see the shoulders of a six-foot-tall human. Of course, this changes slightly, depending on the size of the human and the size of the horse; a weanling can probably only see the torso of the human at close range.

Imagine this from a horse's point of view: A stranger is walking directly toward you. You can see the figure perfectly, but as the figure approaches, the upper and lower extremities rapidly blur and disappear. At six feet of distance, the figure disappears completely. You can no longer see the figure, but you can smell it and hear the strange noises it makes. Then from out of nowhere, a hand appears just six inches in front of your face and touches you. You can see the hand, but the figure that the hand belongs to is invisible, although you can still hear and smell it. Sounds like something out of a horror film. I am always amazed when even the gentlest horse will allow me to pet his forehead while standing in front of him. I hardly ever do because it seems rude to me. If we were to approach the horse from the side or from an angle at the rear, the horse is able to see us the whole time. I do not recommend approaching from the rear.

Often an inexperienced or unstarted horse will raise his head or move around when being bridled or will become nervous when being touched around the chest or the knee area of the front feet. This is because a horse cannot see the rider or handler in these areas. The horse is not trying to be contradictory; he simply can't see what is going on and wants to. The only other blind spot in a horse's field of vision is directly behind the head and directly above the head in a field equal to the width of the horse's head. Of course, with a slight movement, he can see what is in that blind spot; but keep in mind that while on a horse, if you cannot see the horse's eye, he cannot see you, only your legs.

There is really so much more to know about the horse's eye. I can either stop here or go on for several hundred more pages. My hope is that this little bit of knowledge will spark curiosity in the reader and that the reader will springboard off the tiny amount of knowledge written here and go on to do research of their own. I spent well over a year in my early twenties reading about and thinking about the eye of a horse and how it works. The only way any one of us can become better horsemen is to work at it and try to learn.

Hearing and Smell, Taste and Touch

A horse has very good hearing, and this is partially facilitated by the mechanics of the outer ear. A horse can rotate the ear 180 degrees and pick up slight sounds directly in front directly behind and all around. With the combined force of both ears, the horse can pick up sound from 360 degrees around him. Also, both ears work independently, so a horse can listen to sound in front and behind at the same time with great accuracy. Most old-timers said a horse that travels with one ear perked forward and one ear perked back is a smart one. Horses pick up sound frequency at a rate of fifty-five hertz to thirty-five kilohertz compared to a human's fourteen HZ and twenty-five KHZ. They can also hear one octave higher than we can and two lower. The frequency at which a horse hears makes them more sensitive to shrill sounds and deep bass tones. Personally, I try to keep my mouth shut while working a horse because it is impossible to tell if the frequency of my voice bothers them. A horse can pick up sound accurately from as far away as 14,436 feet away all the way around them, two and seven-tenths of a mile. In contrast, a dog can only accurately pick up sound from 1,320 feet, a quarter mile, and a human from 300 feet.

A horse also has a far-more acute sense of smell than a human. The horse has a separate sensory organ that humans do not have. This allows an ability to pick up and discern a scent over one hundred times better than we can. A horse can also detect pheromones to a very high degree. All animals create pheromones that directly correlate to emotion, physical stress, health, and reproductive ability or availability, among other things. Humans can pick up some high levels of pheromones but are almost completely unable to recognize the meanings. Horses, on the other hand, can very acutely understand what pheromones in other horses and other species of mammals represent. Yet another reason why horsemen must learn to control their emotions.

The taste sensory and spectrum of a horse is very similar to that of a human; although a horse is more tolerant of bitter tastes. Sweet, sour, salty, and bitter are tasted at the back of the horse's tongue and the roof of the mouth. The tip of the tongue has very little taste sensory but has a high degree of touch receptors.

Horses have a high concentration of touch receptors at the lips, nose, and around the eyes and have over four billion touch receptors in the mouth alone. The number of sensory receptors on the horse's body varies from a few hundred to thousands per square inch on different parts of the body. Some are sensitive to light only, others to touch only, and some to both. This, of course, varies, depending on age, breed, and color. The figure below shows some of the highly touch-sensitive areas of the horse's body.

OTHER TOOLS IN THE TOOLBOX

A horseman's role in the starting process is to give the horse "tools" that the horse can use to find the answers later in his training. A confident horse will find the "tools" more useful and will be better able to call them to memory later on when the horse needs them. One of the tools that the horseman gives the horse is the knowledge to recognize and properly respond to cues.

When starting a horse, a horseman uses a specific cue in order to create a specific reaction from the horse. A horseman sets up a horse to succeed by creating a scenario where the only reasonable reaction that the horse can think of is the reaction desired by the horseman. By setting a horse up to succeed, the horseman creates a correspondence between specific cues and specific desired reactions. A horse that has been advanced in this manner will begin to start looking for specific and consistent cues from the horseman that correspond to specific and consistent reactions from himself so he can properly maintain his role in the relationship. Throughout the horse's life, he will remain vigilant in search of cues. This will eventually result in a soft and fluid trained horse.

A horseman keeps in mind and designs his efforts based on the knowledge that between himself and the horse, the horseman is the only one that knows what is going on and why. Knowing that the horse does not understand what is expected gives the horseman the power to prevent the horse from correlating undesired reactions with cues. If the horse does not react to a cue in the manner that the horseman had intended, the horseman can simply set up the horse again and again with the same cue until the horse reacts in the desired manner. The horseman knows that horses do not learn from pressure but from the release of pressure; when the horse responds correctly, the horseman releases the pressure, and the horse learns. The un-started horse is clueless at this point with regard to what is going on and what is expected of him. Horses get scared when they don't know how they are supposed to behave but gain confidence from knowing their role in events and what is expected of them.

When starting a horse, the horseman proceeds slowly with a detailed plan that allows each event to segue into the next with specific desired actions and reactions. These coordinated events have been painstakingly and methodically thought out so that each event in a series of events or movements play out like well-rehearsed ballet. The horseman plans the horse's actions for the day so that by moving, the horse learns to bend; by bending, the horse learns to balance; and by balancing, the horse gains confidence and wants to move more. This takes a keen understanding of the horse and his physical capabilities and is a lifelong venture for the horseman.

A good horseman directs the start of a horse in a manner that allows coordinated events to take place. By starting a horse in a directed or coordinated manner, the horseman can remain in control of what happens to the horse and how the horse will react. The horse, in turn, is never left in doubt as to how he should behave and never loses confidence but gains confidence exponentially. An example of this is an exercise of pulling a horse around the back of the saddle. The horseman puts the right snaffle-bit rein behind the back of the cantle or across the seat of the saddle and makes contact, or pulls on the rein, from the left side of the horse. By standing on the left side and making contact on the right, the horseman engages the pressure from the proximity of his body to direct the horse in the desired direction of the contact. In order to follow his head, the horse must move forward. In order to move forward, the horse must bend and turn. In order to maintain forward motion, the horse must balance his body and remain inline. By finding balance in the maneuver, the horse gains confidence about how he is expected to react. In this way, the horseman has set up the horse to be confident about a maneuver before adding the weight of the rider so that when the horse tries to move with more weight and less balance than before, he will know that it can be done. The series of events left the horse with only one clear way to react, therefore setting up the clear understanding of how to react to the next event. A very talented horseman can direct the first encounter with a horse to influence the actions of a horse years in the future.

A horseman that starts a horse with specifics and design, always setting a horse up to succeed in events that coordinate with the following events and successes, creates a new environment in the horse's thinking. In this environment, specific cues produce specific actions without variation. By the horse's reckoning the reaction desired by the horseman is the only possible thing the horse can do. When taught this way, a horse will discontinue the search for a way out or a lazy way of doing work. The horse will do the work as he was taught, not because it is the only way he knows how but rather because he thinks that it is the only thing that can be done. The horse does not know that he can fight or refuse; he believes that he must react in the manner he has been shown. Once this stage has been reached, the horse is started and is prepared to learn through training. The next book in the series of the art of horsemanship is titled *The Next Three Years* and picks up where this book ends, explaining in detail the steps taken to balance, collect, and athleticized the horse in the years that follow the starting process. After several years of training, the horse is prepared to be finished, which is the final book, *The Finished Horse.*

CLASSICAL TRAINING

Bodily exercise, when compulsory, does no harm to the body; but knowledge which is acquired under compulsion obtains no hold on the mind.

—Plato

Classical training in any of the many disciplines of horsemanship focuses on building and balancing a horse that works because he has learned to love work and executes maneuvers with the highest degree of precision and harmony that can be physically achieved. By using the methods of classic horsemanship, the horse's usefulness and ability are prolonged through fitness and precision in the movement. A classically trained horse is balanced, limber, collected, and can maneuver with great efficiency at low or high speed. Very few classical training methods are used in the horse world today because results can be achieved faster and easier through the methods of natural horsemanship, which is a method of using the horse's natural inclinations to guide the horse through maneuvers. Unfortunately, the highest degree of precision and balance in a horse cannot be got in this manner. Classic training is slow and methodical, with each step advancing the horse and opening the door for the next step to come. Through natural horsemanship, the very best natural athletes rise to the top without the aid of training but are more often than not injured by their own athleticism because the horse has not been taught how to move. Natural horsemanship practices are based off the horse's compulsions; however, what a horse does under compulsion, he does without thinking. The only way to change the way a horse thinks is to change the way he moves through the art of classic training methods.

THE HORSEMAN'S EMOTIONS

Maturity is achieved when a person postpones
immediate pleasures for long term values.

—Joshua L. Liebman

In horsemanship, one's expectations govern the outcome of an event. This is especially true when starting a horse. An un-started horse does not know what is expected of him and will therefore take cues of expected behavior from anywhere he can. A trained horse has learned to discern between the emotions and thoughts that the rider is expressing that pertain to him. The trained horse will react to the cues he gets from the rider's thoughts and emotions that pertain to him and filter those that are not pertinent to him. The unstarted horse, or one that has just begun training, does not know how to decipher the thoughts and emotions of a human and act in accordance to all of them. There is no black magic or mumbo jumbo involved here. It's not that a horse can read our mind; humans tend to wear our emotions on our sleeve and express much of our thought and continence through body language. Humans are the only animals that can consider the future, and often our consideration of future events disturbs and confuses the young horse that is able only to focus on the present.

Humans have a developed spoken language, and because of this, we as a species have become dull to communication through body language. Horses, however, are masters at reading body language and learn very quickly to read humans as well as they read other horses. Since a horse cannot use abstract thought, he is left to assume that every emotion and thought he reads in a human's body language pertains to him. For centuries horsemen have said that horses sense fear and become nervous themselves, and in a way it's true; a horse can read your fear of him through your body language. The horse has no idea what you are afraid of, only that you are afraid. The horse that reads fear on a human starts to look for whatever it is that a human is afraid of for the sake of his self-preservation. This is true of all our emotions. A horse can read the confidence on a human just as well as the fear.

A horseman that starts horses and begins their training has a developed ability to gain and maintain absolute control of his own thoughts and emotions and is not bridled by time. In this manner, he is able to direct and influence the thoughts and emotions of his horse through the regulation of his own emotions. A horseman does not allow a horse to know if the horseman is angry, worried, in a hurry, etc., because of the detrimental effects that can be caused by transparent emotions. The horseman schedules the work to be done so that the horse's needs are never in competition with the clock.

GROUNDWORK

Take time but never waste it.

—Billy Arthur

The preparations or groundwork on a young horse need not exceed the work the horse will be exposed to in the thirty days that follow the preparation. As an example, there is no need to practice swinging a rope on a two-year-old colt that a horseman has no intention of roping off of until the end of the third year. If a horse is going to be hobbled, he needs to be prepared for the hobbles; if a horse is going to be saddled and ridden, he needs to be prepared for a saddle and rider. Preparing a horse for an action or maneuver that he is not physically or mentally mature enough for or will never conceivably be exposed to is a misuse of time. Time is spent more wisely working a horse at a level he is physically and mentally mature enough for and making preparations only for the next step in the starting or training process. Skipping steps or moving ahead out of order is wasteful on behalf of the horseman and confusing to the horse. There is no reason in the world that a horse should be schooled in all his groundwork at once. The horseman can groundwork the horse in preparation for the first thirty rides then go back and groundwork the horse again for the next thirty, etc. For me, it is not uncommon to bring a horse into the round pen and do preparatory work or remedial groundwork for several years after the horse has been started. Better horsemen than me find ways to improve the horse through groundwork for the entirely of the horse's life.

Groundwork that is aimed at gentling a horse, e.g., join up, liberty, and similar methods, are for the benefit of the horseman, not the horse. Many of these types of work that take aim at building a relationship between horse and rider are actually designed to build and strengthen the trust the rider has in the horse. Many horsemen use these types of exercises with great results. It is important that the horseman never forgets that the work the horse is doing is an effort to inspire confidence in the rider by showing that the horse is willing and thoughtful in his movement. A horseman must be very honest with himself at these times because it is easy to sour a horse on repetitive work that does not offer mental stimulation.

Some horses are quiet enough that they will allow a rider to skip ahead. The time and effort are wasted though; if a horse will allow it today, he will allow it tomorrow or next week or six months from now when the work is supposed to be introduced. Time should be spent mastering skills in each level in its own time rather than jumping ahead to see how much the horse will stand for. Other horses will not allow any skipping ahead, and no amount of training sweating, beating, or cursing will make them. Time is wasted when a horseman tries to teach a horse something that the horse is not physically or mentally mature enough for, and the horseman runs a huge risk of souring the horse in the process. The horse will learn the maneuver perfectly in its due time and never before. A horseman is lucky if he can learn this without ruining a horse.

A horseman that has a plan for a horse's start, with specific benchmarks of skill with regard to time, will never run the risk of souring a horse because of rushing it and will never have to go back and redo anything because his horse will progress by small, measured, and designed increments every time the horse is worked. A horseman that works in this way rarely impresses anyone with regard to how quickly he can start a horse; however, he generally rides a better finished horse than his contemporaries that let or ask a horse to do too much before the horse is ready.

Use Time

> *Someone is sitting in the shade today because some-*
> *one planted a tree a long time ago.* (Warren Buffet)

Each step of the horse's training should take as long as the horse needs to learn what is being asked. Sometimes the horseman misjudges the amount of time needed but never allows this to hurry him or the horse or the work. If it takes four minutes or four days for the horse to learn to correctly walk around the pen, then that is the time that must be taken. The horseman knows that the horse has mastered the skill when the horse moves with fluid confidence. The horse will ask for more when he is ready. Horses have an artful way of asking for more work, and because each horse is different, there is no way to write exactly how a horse will ask. I am not a good-enough wordsmith to craft a sentence that properly explains how a horse asks without using vague language and implications of magic. If a horseman observes closely, the horseman will see and come to understand the way individual horses communicate. With time, the horseman will learn to see how most horses want to communicate. The goal is to learn how all horses want to communicate. None have. Some horsemen are shackled to the idea; others are happily married to it.

The horseman has wasted time if he asks the horse to trot or lope before the horse can walk with balance and rhythm. A horse can be pushed in a variety of ways to do a variety of things but cannot learn or advance when being pushed past its mental or physical maturity level. Nothing is uglier to the horseman than seeing a young horse willingly do a maneuver incorrectly or unwillingly doing a maneuver to the best of its ability. The willingness of a horse has sealed its fate as a ward to a human; this stewardship must be taken with the greatest of gravity.

Overstimulating to the point of acceptance is also an example of time-wasting. The horse should be expected to tolerate the movements, actions, and stimuli of the horseman and nothing more. Waving chainsaws around and popping bullwhips while standing on the young horse's back are a ridiculous waste of time. Showmanship is an art like any other. Showmanship at the expense of a horse's mental well-being is abuse.

On a fairly regular basis, I find myself second-guessing parts of my program and thinking to myself that one or more sequences in a series of actions in my training program could or should be cut out. Over the years I have cut out a lot of fat in my work that was really a waste of time, but I have also added a lot of small simple steps that have greatly improved my horses and made my entire program more efficient. Often the very small, very simple steps that look like the horse is getting or learning nothing from and seem like a step taken for the sake of taking it actually prove to be the most useful. It is very hard for a horseman to watch a horse work and really tell for sure if the horse is learning or gaining confidence or better control of their own body, and it is impossible if the horseman has little understanding; however, for me I have found that the very easy and very simple steps are the ones the horse learns best from.

HORSES AND HORSEMEN

*They say princes learn no art truly but the Art of
Horsemanship. The reason is the brave beast is no flatterer,
he will throw the prince as soon as his groom.*

—Ben Jonson

A horse's thinking is powered entirely by the horse's ego. This is to say that a horse thinks with the movement of its body. Horses are designed to be in nearly constant movement, and their organs, sensory as well as internal, operate at optimal levels when the body is in motion. When moving, the horse's brain secretes the highest levels of serotonin; blood flow, oxygen levels, and sensory systems yield greater efficiency. In fact, a horse takes in and processes information best when moving. Further, the horse's movement and the ease or difficulty he has in movement have a direct correlation on the horse's emotions. Freedom of movement feels comfortable to a horse; difficulty in movement feels uncomfortable. A horse thinks of himself only and what feels comfortable or uncomfortable. Since the horse has no ability for abstract thought (at this stage), he cannot conceive that hard work equals a payoff in the future. He can only understand what he is feeling right now. The horse identifies entirely with the physical body and its wants. Any thinking that is not "I" or "me" is abstract to a horse. Abstract thought is difficult for a horse. No horse has ever looked at another horse being ridden and projected himself into the same situation. The horseman, on the other hand, while he may be an egotist, is systematically thinking about the wants and needs of another (the horse). The desire to make another individual better is what drives the horseman. He is thinking far into the abstract, designing the horse's future years in advance. It is important for the horseman to remember that he and the horse are driven by two entirely different goals. When the horseman learns to use the horse's ego as a training tool, he will find that the horse learns to move with balance and rhythm, constantly advancing because it feels more comfortable. Art for the sake of art.

THE PSYCHOLOGY OF GROUNDWORK

We can't do good work if we don't know why we are doing the work.

A horseman does whatever kind and as much groundwork as is necessary to give him the confidence to step on the horse and ride off. The kind of groundwork done and the amount of groundwork done have very little effect on the horse's mental preparedness because the horse has no idea what is going on or why. The horse does not know he is being started and will eventually be trained. Groundwork is a time for the horseman to observe the horse and his reactions so that he (the horseman) has the confidence to proceed and pass that confidence on to the horse. During groundwork and into the first rides, the horse is forced to take at face value the horseman's opinions as to whether or not the two are properly prepared. If the horseman is confident that the horse is ready for the next stage in the starting process, the horse will agree to be confident as well because the horse does not know what the next step is.

The horse's thinking is ego. He believes that he is an expert at whatever he does seconds after he first tries it. Horses do not consider degrees of difficulty or sloppy work versus clean work. The horse does not compare himself to other horses that perform maneuvers better than he. The horse cannot remember learning a maneuver and perfecting it. A horse knows that he cannot perform a maneuver when it is first introduced and knows that he can after he has done it once. A horse cannot consider being ready or not being ready for a maneuver or to advance; this is up to the horseman. Reading a horse during groundwork gives the horseman the confidence to advance the horse. Whatever type of groundwork and however much a horseman needs to feel confident are what should be done because the horseman's confidence is all that matters to the horse.

All groundwork serves to instill confidence in the horseman that the horse can be ridden or perform a specific maneuver safely. Different styles of groundwork serve to suit different confidence levels and the psychological necessities of different horsemen. From the perspective of the horse, there is no such thing as bad or useless groundwork so long as nothing is done to scare or hurt the horse. Groundwork can be used to "pre-teach" a maneuver; however, the horse can only be as confident and mentally prepared as the horseman when the time comes to actually learn the maneuver.

The only forms of groundwork that are purely for the benefit of the horse are those that are designed to strengthen and balance the horse, increase elasticity and suspension, and generally further athleticize the horse. The majority of the groundwork I do is *after* the first twenty or thirty rides and is designed specifically to strengthen and athleticize the horse. Doing this work after I have ridden the horse allows me to retain the upper hand in terms of knowledge of how the horse moves. This is to say that for the first twenty or thirty rides, I understand how and why the horse moves better than he does, if for no other reason than I have started several thousand head and the horse, in any given situation, has never been started before, so it is all new to him. I take full advantage of this knowledge of how a horse moves and why, using it to keep both the horse and myself safe. I see no reason to allow a horse to fully understand the scope of his strength, speed, and endurance while I instill confidence in his very fragile mind. Once a horse has gained a degree of confidence about carrying a rider and having his balance and movement manipulated, then he can start to learn how to use his strength and speed. Most forms of groundwork do this to some degree, but many do not benefit the horse at all.

Forms of groundwork that scare, or hurt, a horse are detrimental to the horse in the starting process, as well as any other level of training. Anything that scares a horse to the point that he feels the need to defend himself, anything that physically hurts the horse, and anything that leaves the horse by itself to "figure it out on its own" is detrimental and should be considered abuse rather than work.

Groundwork is preparatory work. If a horseman has scared a horse in the groundwork, he has only prepared the horse to be scared. If a horseman physically hurts the horse in groundwork, he has prepared the horse to hurt. In all forms of groundwork, the horseman must maintain control of the horse and the stimuli. Loss of control of either will cause a wreck that scares or hurts the horse. Maintaining control induces the horse to look to the horseman for insight as to how he should react. The horseman that maintains control creates a horse that will always look to him for guidance. The horseman that leaves a horse to "figure it out on his own" creates a horse that will, and the horseman has no control over what the horse figures out. Most often a horse that has been taught to deal with situations on his own will do so by spooking and running off. Remember that method has worked for the horse for eons.

Any form of preparation that is designed to or is done to the point that the horse ignores stimuli will make the horse harder to train and more likely to spook and run off in the future. Flagging or sacking a horse out past the point of tolerance to the point of acceptance or hanging things like tarps off the horse are examples. Through training, a horse learns to focus on work and does not spook because he is focused. Through abuse, a horse is taught to ignore stimuli. Once a horse has learned to ignore a plastic sack, he can easily learn to ignore a cue from a bit or spur.

Horses have a tendency to spontaneously recover from habituation or desensitizing while they tend to re-habituate very quickly; the method is very difficult to depend on. Classic conditioning (Pavlov) and negative reinforcement (pressure and release) work very well. Positive reinforcement and operant conditioning work well later in the training process, but the un-started horse must be reinforced every time.

A horse thinks when moving freely but does not think at all when forced to "take it." This is why the horseman strives for tolerance in a horse, but not acceptance. A horse that has been forced into or worked until he accepts something has completely turned off the thought processes. A horse is happy and confident when moving in balance and often moves undesirably when searching for balance. A young horse will often grab and run or even buck several times under saddle in a search for balance in the way he is being asked to move. A young horse that bucks under saddle is not a bad horse; he is a horse trying to find an answer.

Many horsemen use bitting up, back, down, or around or several combinations to prepare a horse to be guided with the snaffle bit or hackamore before riding. Out of habit, I call all methods "bitting up" regardless of whether I mean back around or down. All forms have great advantages as well as great disadvantages that can either advance or retard the advancement of the young horse. Very few horsemen are "tied hard and fast" to a system of preparing a young horse for guidance in this manner, as what can be most advantageous to one horse can be of the greatest disadvantage to another. Unfortunately, trial and error is the system most horsemen have used to gain the experience to effectively prescribe what and how much an individual horse needs. There is no greater teacher than experience; nevertheless, the horse pays the tuition. When planning the method of bitting up that is to be used, a horseman takes into consideration the temperament of the horse and the physical ability of the horse. The different mechanics of bitting up are also to be considered and compared to the conformation of the horse. Any and all forms of bitting up will cause a horse to put more weight on the forehand if overused. Since the underlying drive of all horsemanship is to further collect the horse by training the horse to shift the center of balance and carriage of weight onto the hindquarters, a horseman is judicial in the use of bitting up.

FOUNDATION

When the whirlwind passes, the wicked is no more,
but the righteous has an everlasting foundation.

—Proverbs 10:25

When starting a horse, the horseman keeps in mind that the work he does today is work that he will not have to do tomorrow. This is why starting a horse is often referred to as foundation work. A house built on a solid foundation needs only to be built once while a house built on a flawed foundation is constantly crumbling at the stress points and must be rebuilt. A horseman keeps this in mind, knowing that a horse will retain the knowledge from his starting whenever he is stressed or confused. Later in training, no matter the situation or complexity of a maneuver, a horseman can break a maneuver down to a simpler form that the horse is more comfortable with that was learned in the starting process and continue teaching the horse without causing distress to the horse's mind. The simplest form that work can be broken down to is the "go, stop, turn" that the horse discovered when learning to learn in the starting process. The horseman strives to build a foundation of knowledge for a horse that is based on going, stopping, and turning because this foundation can be adapted to fit any situation that the horse and the horseman may face later in training. A horseman shies from patterning the horse and instilling ideas through constant repetition because a learned pattern only fits within the boundaries of that particular pattern. A patterned horse must be retaught from the ground up every new maneuver while a horse that has a solid foundation can use the knowledge he has gained to advance exponentially. Consistency should never be confused with patterning; consistency is doing a thing the same way every time while patterning is doing a thing over and over. A horseman strives to balance a horse through consistency, not shape a horse to fit a pattern through repetition.

Patterning and the Use of Patterns

To understand is to perceive patterns.

—Isaiah Berlin

Many horsemen use patterns to practice and introduce maneuvers to a horse. The practice works well because horses love patterns. Patterns appeal to a horse's fragmented thought process because they know once a sequence has started exactly what is expected of them through the duration of the sequence and when the sequence ends. The sequence of a pattern puts the fragmented thoughts of a horse into line and makes thinking inline very easy and pleasing for a horse. Horses love to figure out patterns and practice them. The use of patterns can be a very important tool to a horseman. Through the pattern, he can refine and balance the horse's movement without confusing the horse because the horse will not break a known pattern once the sequence has started. Since horses are so receptive to patterns, a horseman must also be very careful with the use of the pattern because he can easily and unintentionally pattern the horse. Patterning the horse is practicing all the maneuvers of an exercise from beginning to end over and over and using repetition to frame the horse within the pattern rather than teaching the horse balance and refinement within the maneuver. Patterning a horse can be very dangerous and detrimental to the training process because once a horse is patterned, any change in the pattern can scare and frustrate the horse because he no longer understands how he is expected to behave. Most patterning is done in the years after the horse has been started, and if the horse has been started correctly and has a firm foundation in his understanding, the horse can be brought back to a high level of performance. If, however, the horse has been started through patterning, then it can be very difficult to rebuild the confidence in the horse. In order to keep from patterning the horse, the horseman uses exercises to practice the maneuvers within a pattern rather than practicing the whole pattern repeatedly. A consistent horseman that uses patterns can develop a versatile horse that is able to adapt to changes and deviations within the pattern while a rider that uses patterning to train a horse runs the risk of developing a horse that relies on the pattern itself to instill confidence and method in the work.

It is ridiculous to think that a horse learns through repetition; however, many people try to teach a horse by repeating a maneuver over and over. I say that trying to teach a horse through repetition is ridiculous because no other mammal on earth learns well through repetition, so there is no reason to think that a horse would be the exception. All mammals, horses, and humans as well learn most efficiently through variation. There must be consistency in what is correct and what is not correct; however, the circumstances of what is being taught and learned must be varied in order for the horse to gain a clear understanding of the principle. For instance, the horse cannot improve the haunch turn by setting up for the turn and then turning thirty or forty revolutions in a row. The horse can improve the haunch turn by setting up and turning two or three revolutions then setting up and turning another then walking a straight line and setting up and turning some more. By using variation, the horseman lets the horse find the best way to set himself up and use his body in a manner that is efficient and nontaxing. The horse may still end up doing thirty haunch turns, but he does not do them all at once. Of course, a haunch turn is an advanced maneuver that is not the concern of a horseman or a horse in the starting process; however, it is an easy example. So often I see young horses being subject to hours of repetitive, nonessential garbage. The riders that do this sort of work often say things like "Seems like I have to restart this horse every day," and "Well, the tough ones always turn out the best." In truth, it is not that the horse is "tough" or is not learning; it is that the horse has learned that the work is boring and does not like it. If the work is boring for the rider, it is boring for the horse. The young horse must have mental stimulation. For a young horse being started, three or four segments of go, stop, and turn done with a degree of finesse from the horse should be enough for the horseman to scratch the young horse on the neck and put him away until tomorrow.

OF HORSES AND HORSEMEN

<hr>

*That horse ain't worried about you trying to eat
him, he's figuring on a way to eat you.*

—Troy Barnett

Horses do not fear humans because we are predators. To say they do
suggests that horses have collective genetic memories that tell them
that ancient humans ate horse flesh. If this was so, horses would also
be afraid of barn cats. If horses had collective genetic memory, they
would also collectively remember that humans have ridden and cared
for them for thousands of years. Horses fear what we tell them to
fear through our body language. A horseman must be careful that he
does not use body language to communicate to a horse that he (the
horseman) is something the horse should fear.

Like all mammals, horses are predisposed to keep a distance
between themselves and things that they do not understand. Horses
are individuals with preferences to individual space. Horses do not
like their space being trespassed upon by foreign objects or other
animals. Horses do not like other animals encroaching on them and
will move away from the other animal to prevent that from happening. Horses are private animals with their own social structure and
do not like unknown people putting hands on them. Horses are only
afraid of a person if the person is doing something scary. It is a horseman's responsibility to know if what he is doing is or will be scary
to a horse. The horseman knows he is a predator and knows that he

moves and acts like a predator and should know that any horse with any sense will move away from a predator, not because the horse is scared but because he doesn't want to be scared. A horseman must keep in mind that the horse does not know why he has been caught, why he is being ridden, or what he is being prepared for. The horse cannot conceive that if he performs at a high level, he will be retired and stand at stud. If he did, you can bet he would meet you at the gate every morning!

The horseman is responsible for making sure everything that he does to the horse is conceivable to the horse. A horse will never do something to you; he does things because of you. The horse does not care about the horseman's feelings. The horse only cares about his own feelings. The horse will not and cannot relate to you nor can you ever really relate to him. This is a hard-line stance that is very hard for a lot of horse lovers to swallow; however, it is true. Many times in my life, having this point of view has caused some heated discussions that seem to cause other people to think that I don't like horses. This could not be further from the truth. In my opinion, being honest about a horse and how he thinks and acts makes it easier to do good work. As horsemen, our canvas is an ever-changing medium that we can in no way really ever understand. At some point, the best we can do is care about the well-being of the horse and hope for the best.

Thinking About the Work

The world is full of people that never bothered to open the box their brain came in, unwrap it, read the directions, and use the darn thing.

If I were to ask you, the reader, to do a backflip, you would likely tell me you can't. Through verbal persuasion or physical violence, I may get you to try, but you would try with the belief that the act cannot be done. There is a better than average chance that you will be hurt when you try. If you are an individual with extraordinary athletic ability, you may be able to do a backflip; but since you do not know how to do a backflip, there is still a high chance that you will injure yourself. If, however, I spend the time teaching you all the exercises that will prepare your body to do a backflip and teach you the mechanics of the movements, you will be able to do a backflip with ease and confidence and greatly reduce the odds of being injured in the maneuver. Every new thing we ask a horse to do is like asking for a backflip. The horse cannot help but think that what is being asked is impossible. He can be persuaded to try the impossible but will very likely injure himself in trying. The horseman has a responsibility to the horse in knowing what is and what is not possible for the horse and why; the horseman also has the responsibility of teaching the horse how to do something before he asks the horse to do it.

Linear Thought and Nonlinear or Fragmented Thought

We live in the mind, in ideas, in fragments. We no longer drink in the wild outer music of the streets—we remember only.

—Henry Miller

One of the underlying difficulties in man's relationship to horses is that we two animals think differently. This very definite difference in our thought process also lends to the difficulty man has in understanding or relating to a horse and what he does. The vast majority of humans, and by proxy, the vast majority of horsemen, have a linear thought process. Linear thinking is a process of thought following known cycles or step-by-step progression where a response to a step must be elicited before another step is taken. This means that we humans think in straight lines; our ability to think in a straight line leads to our ability to think in the abstract and think in terms of future time and space. The sequential order of the number sequence one through ten is a linear idea. The conception of this linear thought leads to the conception of one through a billion or trillion or any other conceivable number. A horse cannot do this. Nonlinear or fragmented thought is the mind relating similar things and experiences. Horses' minds do not naturally think in straight lines. Rather, their thought consists of associations spanning out from many different connecting points. A horse can see the difference between one and ten but cannot tell that the difference is nine. To a horse, the difference between one and ten is the same difference as between one and ten billion. This is why horses love patterns, because it helps them to understand differences. Through consistency in our work, a horse can learn sequences and grasp linear ideas, but will never see the world the way we do. Because of the way horses think, it should be no surprise that they are excited or caught off guard by the things we do, or that they spook and shy from seemingly invisible ghosts. It takes a long time for a horse to learn the pattern of being caught, brushed, saddled, and ridden while for the human it is the "same old, same old." This is why consistency is so important in a horse's start and training.

Fragmented or nonlinear thought applies to a horse's concept of time as well. Time is an abstract idea, and something only humans rely on. A horse does not mark the hours between 7:00 a.m. and 7:00 p.m. The horse knows he is hungry at 7:00 p.m. but cannot remember being hungry that morning. He knows he is hungry, but not what time it is. Monday, Wednesday, Friday means nothing to the horse, and he does not care to know. All the horses in my barn know that when they hear the four-wheeler start, it is feed time. The horses know because they associate the sound of the motor with getting fed. If it is seven, or seven thirty, they don't know or care. If I am consistent about starting the four-wheeler at seven, the horses will learn the pattern and start banging around in the stalls at seven or even six fifty. Not because the horse knows time but because he knows the pattern. A very consistent horseman will start to develop linear thought in a horse long before he ever starts to work the horse.

Coincidentally, my oldest child just stumbled blurry-eyed into the kitchen; that means it is time for me to feed him then head to the barn and get started because it is almost seven.

Time is known to a horse in fragments of specific events, in order of importance to an individual horse. It should be no surprise that a horse spooks at a leaf on the ground or unfamiliar noise because the horse associates a similar event to something scary or dangerous that has happened in the past. For all we know, it could have been three weeks after his birth or three days ago. This is why a horse having confidence in the horseman's judgment is so important because he is constantly deferring to the experience and assumed prowess of the horseman. Everything we ask a horse to do he thinks is impossible until he tries it. Once a horse has tried, he has no idea that he ever couldn't. A horse depends on the horseman to convince him that a thing can be done.

Because a horse thinks in fragments, the only way to change a horse's mind about something is to fill the horse's memory with the fragmented thoughts that we want him to recall and literally outnumber the fragments of thought we don't want the horse to recall. Oftentimes a horse will stop midstride and study a situation. The horse will hold stock still for a moment or two before making a decision about what is to be done next. This is always a scary moment for a horseman on a young horse because the horse may bolt or may take a deep breath and go on. What is actually happening at these times is that the horse has seen, smelled, heard, or felt something that has conjured up a memory. We horsemen may never know what the thing was; in that moment the horse goes through the entire catalog of its memory, trying to find similarities between what is going on at present and what the horse has experienced in the past. If the horse comes up with a memory that has similar circumstances that resulted in fear or pain on the horse's part, the horse will bolt before the opportunity for fear and pain can result. If the memory with the closest similarities turns out to be benign, then the horse will proceed. Imagine falling through life this way. It is no wonder that the horse has gained a reputation of being flighty and afraid. Through the investment of time, the horseman can override all the horse's memory by creating so many fragments of recollection in the horse's mind where the end result was that the horseman was near and everything turned out all right that eventually the horse will think of the horseman as the common denominator in all good things and will always defer to the judgment of the horseman. When a horseman strives to create a relationship between himself and the horse that is based on partnership and equality, he will find the horse to be a dangerous partner that is always looking out for himself and no one else. If the horseman strives to create a relationship based on the horse's dependence on the horseman, he will find he is a steward to a ward that is loyal, brave, and trusting. Horsemanship is neither slavery nor a partnership; it is a stewardship with great responsibility and great reward.

Dominant and Submissive Behavior

Be careful what you say, they will believe you even if you don't.

—Tony Durrer

Dominance is not a character trait in horses but a behavioral phenomenon. This means that dominance is a secondary effect or by-product that arises from but does not causally influence a process in particular. Mental events in the brain are an epiphenomenon in the sense that they can be caused by physical events in the brain but cannot cause physical events in the brain. For the purposes of this book, "causally" can be thought of as cause and effect. In this way, dominance is caused by a horse's knowledge and past experiences or what he thinks but does not cause what the horse thinks.

If, for instance, a number of horses that do not know each other are put to pasture together, and only one of the horses knows where the feed and water are in that pasture, that horse will be the dominant personality by default for a time. Later the social hierarchy may change, and the role of dominance may fall to a faster or more-athletic horse. Still the dominance is a by-product of the horse's other traits. For dominance to be a character trait, the character in question must have abstract thought and a vision for the situation. The dominant thinker is the horseman, not the horse. With all horses, any character in any situation will gain dominance if that character knows (or pretends to know) more than the others. A horse does not want to be dominant in any situation. A horse will only ever be dominant by default of knowing what is going on better than any other character in the situation. A horse will willingly submit to a horseman if the horseman shows that he has a clear understanding of what is happening and why; however, a horse will grudgingly take the dominant role (because someone has to) if no other horse or horseman will take the responsibility of being dominant. The horse feels safe and comfortable when another horse or the horseman takes the dominant role in a relationship but will always take the responsibility himself if no other will because someone must be dominant. The horseman is responsible for taking on the role of dominance immediately for the sake of the horse's safety and well-being. Remember, the horse does not know what is going on or why and will hurt himself and those around him if he is forced to make decisions regarding things he cannot conceive.

Dominance should never be confused with aggressive behavior. Aggressive behavior is almost always caused by fear. This is true for both the horse and the horseman.

Parsimonious Behavioral

*Porque no observas con cuidado? Why
don't you observe carefully?*

—said in one form or another by every old man
I ever knew when I asked a question

Parsimonious means frugal. Parsimonious behavior can best be explained by a theory called Occam's razor. The theory states, "The assumptions introduced to explain a thing must not be multiplied beyond necessity," or the concept that is the simplest explanation for a phenomenon or behavior is the best one. Horses are ruled by parsimonious behavior and think parsimoniously. The horse will do that which seems to him the simplest and will come to conclusions based on what seems to him most simple. A horseman uses Occam's razor whenever dealing with a horse and considers the horse's actions and reactions based on what the simplest explanation for the behavior may be. A horseman also directs all interaction with the horse to blend seamlessly with the horse's parsimonious behavior. All too often humans attempt to seek out and apply the most abstract conclusions to the behavior of the world around them instead of seeking the simplest and most direct answer first. This tendency is frustrating and confusing to the horse in training and slows the advancement of the horse and his understanding of the horseman.

TROPISM

It has to start someplace. It has to start sometime. What better place than here, what better time than now?

—Zack de la Rocha

Tropism is defined as the turning or bending of a living organism toward or away from external stimulus. Tropism is an involuntary orientation that involves turning or curving into or away from external stimulus and is either a positive or negative response to the source of the stimulus. It is also known as an innate tendency, natural inclination, or propensity to act in a certain manner. When speaking of horses, we are dealing with thigmotropism in specific, which is movement in response to touch, contact, or proximity. Thigmotropism is commonly referred to as a horse's "flight or fight" instinct. In general terms, a horse will choose to move away from external stimulus whenever possible; we think of this as flight. A horse will only choose to move into external stimulus when the opportunity to move away has been taken. This is known as fight. Unfortunately, most humans fail to recognize when a horse is moving into the external stimulation. When working a horse in a round pen or any other enclosure, the opportunity for tropism to cause a horse to move away or fly has been taken away, so tropism causes the horse to move into or fight the stimulation or presence of the horseman. Since the horse is moving around the pen, it seems that the horse is moving away from pressure; however, once the horse realizes that the pressure is not lessening and he is not actually getting away, he starts to push into the pressure. In this example, the movement toward the external stimulus starts with the eye and ear of the horse moving toward the

74

source of the stimulus, the horseman. If the horse changes directions, he will turn toward the source rather than away from it. With time, the tropism will act hand in hand with the satellite movement of the horse, and the horse will be drawn closer and closer to the source of stimulus. Tropism is why "join up" type training works; it is how cutting horses are trained and how cart and draft horses work. Tropism is also the motive behind a horse "pulling back" on a lead rope. In fact, the horse is pushing into the halter at the poll. A horseman must understand tropism and the way it works to properly train a horse and understand that anytime the horse is confined, in any manner, his instinct will be to move into the stimulus. Many methods use the horse's tropism to pattern the horse through repetition because a horse will naturally move into pressure in a specific manner. Exercises can be directed to condition a horse to react in a given manner. When training a horse in an artful manner, the horseman must deal with tropism and condition a horse to go against this involuntary reaction of moving into pressure/stimulus and instead become conditioned to move away from pressure/stimulus. A horse moving into pressure is not really trained; he is simply reacting to the world around him. It is very easy to set a horse up to react to a situation in a manner that makes him looked trained; however, if the horse is taken out of a controlled environment, the rider will no longer have any control. Action taken by compulsion is action taken without thought. The act of conditioning a horse to consider his actions and reactions is the first step a horseman takes in introducing a horse to think linearly instead of fragmentary, to act instead of simply react. By studying the horse and the way he moves and acts, a horseman can learn how tropism works and the way it causes the horse to move and react. Armed with this knowledge, a horseman can swiftly, precisely, and systematically teach a horse.

Understanding how and why a horse thinks, as well as how and why a human thinks, is cardinal to the horseman. The horseman cannot expect the horse to take an extra step for him if he is unwilling to take an extra step for the horse.

THE AIDS

We are born weak, we need strength; helpless, we need aid; foolish, we need reason. All that we lack at birth, all that we need when we come to a man's estate, is the gift of education.

—Jean-Jacques Rousseau

None of the aids can be good or bad, severe or mild in and of themselves. The aids can do nothing on their own, and it is the responsibility of the horseman to understand how to use the aids to benefit and advance the horse.

The aids are the body and the extensions of the horseman's body; they are what the horseman uses to communicate with the horse. The aids are the tools the horseman uses to manipulate the horse's body in terms of speed and direction, space, and time.

The Bit

A golden bit does not make the horse worth more.

For the purposes of this book about starting colts, we shall discuss the snaffle bit and hackamore only because those are the two most common tools for starting a horse; other bits and their uses will be discussed in later volumes.

The snaffle bit is a common tool that can be found anywhere in the world that horses are being trained. It works on a one-to-one pull or zero ratio, meaning that for every pound of pressure the horseman exerts on the reins of the bit, an equal amount of pressure is exerted on the horse's mouth. The snaffle puts pressure on the horse's tongue and the corners of his mouth or lips. With severe misuse, the snaffle can also apply pressure on the sensitive bars of the horse's jaw. The pressure on the tongue comes when the bit is disengaged and is an equal pressure to the weight of the bit. When the snaffle is disengaged, it lays across the horse's tongue. The weight and feel of the bit in the mouth is a relaxing constant to the snaffle-bit horse and gives the horse a sense of security. For this reason, the horseman should never lose direct contact between his hands and the bit because loss of contact results in unintended signals to the horse. When the horseman loses contact with the bit, he also loses the communication of his own confidence to the horse through the bit. When a snaffle is engaged, there is a direct pressure from the horseman's hand to the corner of the horse's cheek. As a horse learns to move away from or give to pressure. He learns to turn his head and neck from this direct pressure. The snaffle literally pulls the horse in a desired direction. The right hand of the horseman turns the horse's head right, and the left hand turns the horse's head left. A snaffle bit should only be pulled on by one rein at a time. If both reins are pulled at the same time, the bit collapses on the joint in the middle, and all contact as well as all engagement is lost; therefore, the cue for the maneuver is lost, and time is wasted, not used. The corners of the horse's mouth are the least sensitive but are still sensitive enough that a horseman can train a horse to work in rapid and efficient fashion by subtle cues from the bit. Snaffle bits are used to start horses because they offer simple and direct cues that are easy for the horse to understand. Misuse of the snaffle bit can result in an injury to the horse's mouth as well as complicate the entire movement of the horse.

Most horsemen are of the opinion that any bit that is jointed or broken in the middle is a form of snaffle; the variations of these are vast, and in this particular discussion, we are speaking only of non-leverage snaffle bits. For the purposes of starting young horses, the most common snaffle is the ring or D-ring snaffle; although the half or full-cheek snaffle is also very common. A ring snaffle is most common with performance-style training, as it offers the most direct signal. A D-ring snaffle is common among cowboys and people that ride with more contact because there is some offer of indirect (pushing rather than pulling) pressure on the opposite cheek, and the horse is less likely to be rubbed raw because of the added distribution of pressure; the same goes for the half and full-cheek snaffles. A loriner (bit maker) can offer more in-depth observations of different snaffles and their strengths and weaknesses. For the purposes of this book, it is sufficient to say that a snaffle bit is a good tool for starting a young horse. I would like to add at this time that all bits and bosals do create some poll pressure through the leverage of the bit rotating in the mouth and leveraging the headstall down on the poll. The bosal is a leverage tool and creates poll pressure whenever the noseband is engaged. The poll pressure from the snaffle and most bosals in the starting process is so slight it need only to be mentioned, as the fine intricacies of the use of poll pressure could take up an entire book in itself. Poll pressure will be discussed at length and in detail in following volumes where the knowledge is more useful for later stages of training.

A snaffle is a useful tool, and its industry is due to the simplicity of its mechanics. A friend of mine that rides English put it this way, "We use a snaffle on young horses because they cannot really be trusted in their youth. With the snaffle, we can put an obstacle in the exuberance of youth." Her term "obstacle" was a polite way of saying, "We can cause enough pain to change the horse's mind." As I mentioned before, a non-leverage snaffle has a zero ratio, not a one-to-one ratio, as some people tend to say, but a one-to-one pull. A one-to-one ratio is that of a seesaw, or in terms of bits, an elevator bit. A bit with a one-to-one ratio has a lot of leverage. With a zero-ratio or one-to-one pull, a snaffle puts the same amount of pressure on the mouth of the horse as is exerted by the hands of the rider. I have done some experimenting with weights and scales and have learned that a rider of average strength like myself can put an enormous amount of pressure on the mouth of a horse. Horsemen bear a great deal of responsibility whenever we work with a horse at any level, and I think it is important to add emphasis to the amount of responsibility a horseman must be burdened with whenever a snaffle bit is being used. Because these writings are supposed to be more about the art within the work rather than a how-to book, it is enough to say that many riders today do not use a snaffle in an artful manner.

Bosal

The hackamore doesn't care about a horse's pedigree.

A bosal or hackamore should never be mistaken for a mechanical hackamore. A mechanical hackamore is a very complex and misunderstood tool, to be used only by judicious hands when absolutely necessary. The bosal is generally attributed to early California Spanish-style horsemanship; however, the use of braided or twisted material for the purpose of guiding a work animal has been around for as long as man has been horseback. A bosal works on indirect pressure in contrast to the direct pressure or pull that comes from a snaffle bit. When the right hand of the rider pulls the horse's head to the right, the left side of the bosal pushes the horse's head to the right and in so doing guides the horse in the desired direction. Unlike the snaffle, the horseman does not maintain direct contact with the bosal, as the bosal itself keeps the maintenance of contact through the design. A horseman does not use a continuous or long pull with a bosal but instead uses a series of bumps to direct the horse in the direction and at the speed desired. Like the snaffle, the bosal does not work properly if both reins are pulled at the same time and will result in a horse that elevates his head or roots his nose when pressure is applied. A bosal is accompanied by a closed rein system called a *macate*. This *macate* is the same twenty-two-foot long piece of rope that is often used with a snaffle and slobber straps for a similar closed rein system. On a bosal the *macate* is tied with a series of turns around the body of the bosal. These turns adjust the length of the bosals body to create a desired speed of signal for individual horses. Many turns shorten the bosal body and create a faster signal; fewer turns create a slower action from the bosal. The mentality of the individual horse as well as the habit of highly active, or less-active hands on the horseman's part, are considered in the adjustment of the bosal. The bosal can also be adjusted to have more effect on the horse vertically or more effect horizontally. This adjustment is done by running the working rein at the top of the wraps nearer the horse's jaw for more horizontal control or at the bottom of the wraps nearer the heel knot of the bosal for more vertical control. I tend to start with my working rein at the top of my wraps, and as the horse advances, the rein can be lowered.

The bosal with a *macate* and a hanger (headstall) make a hackamore. The *macate* should always be the same diameter as the bosal body for proper balance of the release of pressure from the bosal. Sometimes a hackamore is accompanied by a large browband called *tocas ojos* (touch the eyes) and a throat latch system called a *fiador*. The added accouterments change and adjust the speed and signal of the hackamore. The noseband of the bosal, the heel knot, and the material used to construct the bosal also affect the release the bosal gives as well as the speed of the release. As a rule of thumb, shorter nosebands and heavier heel knots make faster, more-precise releases. Traditionally, a bosal is made from twelve strands of braided rawhide or leather with a rawhide core; however, the materials used are not implicit. A five-eighths-inch diameter bosal is generally considered standard for starting horses; however, modern practices of starting horses at two years old have caused many to use smaller diameter bosals on smaller, younger horses. Many detailed books have been written about the use of bosals and hackamores and should be read before considering the use of the tool.

No bit, bosal, or device will stop a horse; bits aren't made to stop a horse. Bits are made for communication between the horseman's mind and the horse's mind.

The horseman must always remember that the horse has four billion nerve endings in the mouth and many large nerve bundles very close to the skin on the horse's face. These nerves can communicate both pain and pleasure. The nerves in the mouth and face are connected to the limbic system of the brain that plays a large role in the motivation, emotions, learning capabilities, and memory of the horse. The limbic system is where the subcortical structures meet the cerebral cortex. In other words, where the thinking part of the brain connects with the instinctive part. The limbic system also supports epinephrine flow, emotional life, and formation of memories. The pleasure systems of the brain connect to the limbic system and directs intentional movement. This is why horsemen invest so much time and effort into learning about bits and bosals because the mouth and face of the horse has so much to do with how the horse learns and thinks. I cannot overstate that the use of a snaffle bit or bosal is more than simply pulling a horse around in a desired direction. During the starting process, the horse can be set up for future success or failure by the use or misuse of the snaffle bit or bosal.

Spurs

Riding without spurs is like hunting without a rifle.

Spurs are very often a misunderstood and misused tool. A spur is designed to manipulate and offer guidance in terms of direction to the horse's barrel. A spur is meant only to signal a horse of a desired directional change and/or push the body of the horse into a specific space. Spurs are not for increasing a horse's speed, punishing a horse, or making him "go." Longer-legged horsemen use longer-shanked spurs because the feet of a long-legged rider hang below the horse's barrel, and the length of the shank makes up the difference lost in contact. Shorter-legged horsemen use shorter-shanked spurs because the heel of a shorter-legged rider is already close to the horse's body, so a longer shank to shave time off of the desired signal is not needed. Rowel diameter is also to be considered. In general terms, larger rowels offer more surface area and a milder signal while smaller rowels get more to the point. Horsemen choose spurs based on a variety of factors, including the style of stirrup used, the style of boot worn, the style of riding, and the mentality of the horse. Personal preference has a role in the horseman's choice in the spur that is used. Most days I ride ten-plus horses a day, and it is not uncommon for me to change spurs several times a day to suit the different horses. A spur offers direct pressure, asking the horse to move away from pressure. In the starting process, the horseman uses the spur to introduce a horse to the concept of moving away from pressure, as a horse will naturally push against pressure. Spurs are basically one-to-one ratio; however, the length of the shank can add a few degrees of pressure. If a horse becomes dull to the spur, it is not from the use of the spur but from the rider not releasing or disengaging the spur when the horse responds. The spur can do nothing on its own; it must be engaged by the rider.

Some horsemen prefer to go slick-heeled when starting colts. I suppose that if one feels that one does not have enough body control to keep from spurring the young horse at the wrong time, then this makes sense to ride without spurs. I have always worn spurs when starting colts, or riding any horse. My theory has always been, if you don't need spurs, don't use them, but it's the pits to need them and not have them. I have noticed in recent years that there is a trend toward riding fully trained horses without spurs to show off that the horse is so well trained the rider has no need for the spur. I cannot understand why a rider would want to retard themselves in this way.

Bat or Quirt

Being as smart as a whip includes knowing when to not use it.

Bats and quirts are a tool a horseman uses to apply direct pressure/signal to a horse's hip or shoulder and are really only extensions of the rider's hand. A bat offers a very precise and light signal while a quirt tends to be somewhat less precise, except when used by someone very familiar with the tool. Both should be well balanced at the precise middle of the limb and have a popper at the end that can be made to create a very loud pop or crack when engaged. The pop of the popper is to startle a young horse into focus, much like a school teacher clapping her hands at the classroom. A horseman never hits the horse with the bat or quirt but uses the tool to balance and guide the young horse at times when the other aids are less effective. In my lifelong career as a horseman, I have learned several times to look for good reason not to use my quirt. I do use a quirt when starting a horse and carry one whenever I use a hackamore.

The Seat

He who placed me in this seat will keep me here. (Elizabeth I)

The seat is the most important of all the aids available to the horseman. With the seat, the horseman can influence the horse's speed and cadence. All the other aids are used for directional control of the horse. With the seat, the horseman literally drives the horse. The term "seat" is in reference to the rider's entire body position from head to toes. A rider with a good seat remains relaxed throughout the body, rides perfectly straight, and maintains balance. Any rigidity in the rider's body will produce rigidity in the horse's body. Crookedness and lack of balance in the rider's body translates to crookedness and lack of balance in the horse. A rider should sit a horse in a manner that if the horse was erased from under the rider, the rider would land on his feet, legs slightly bent at the knees, and standing otherwise perfectly straight up, looking straight ahead. The hands of the rider should be held slightly above and in front of the saddle, and an imaginary straight line should run from the horse's mouth to the rider's hands to the elbow. This straight line runs perpendicular to the straight line that runs from the top of the rider's head through the spine, pelvis, and legs to the heels. Horsemen spend lifetimes building and maintaining a good seat because without perfect control of one's own body, the rider has no chance to properly control the horse's body. A good seat enables the horseman to feel the horse and its movements. A horseman's seat communicates not only the horseman's wishes but also his confidence and emotion as a whole. This line of communication should be one of the paramount considerations for a horseman before introducing concepts to the horse.

In my opinion, having a sloppy seat is like driving a Ferrari while drunk; it is dangerous and disrespectful.

Saddles and Pads

> *The ship in port is safe, but that's not what*
> *ships are built for.* (Grace Hopper)

The saddle and blanket/pad system used on a young horse is extremely important and oftentimes overlooked. To begin with, there is a tendency to use a junk saddle on the young horse for the introduction and first several rides. Youth and lack of experience on the part of the horse leads to an increase in wear and tear on the horseman's equipment, and good saddles are very expensive. However, a poorly made or poorly fitting saddle only increases the stress on a young horse that is already being stressed. The stress that a horseman puts on the young horse during the starting process has been calculated and is controlled by the direction of the horseman. Any stress or discomfort that he cannot calculate or control should be eliminated, if at all possible, thereby increasing his liberty to teach. A good, well-made saddle should be used at all times. It is very difficult to fit a young horse to a saddle because the back of the horse is not mature and because the horse's body changes drastically as a result of the exercise. Part of the horseman's work is to accommodate the horse by using the best fit he can; this may mean having multiple saddles or a designated "colt" saddle that fits a wide variety of young horses.

The pad/blanket system used is also extremely important and can have a huge effect on the horse's comfort and therefore the horse's ability to work and learn. The pad is not intended to act as a cushion for the horse's back. In fact, research shows that using too thick of a pad actually has a detrimental effect because the weight of the saddle and rider is not evenly distributed across the horse's back. A well-made saddle that fits reasonably well will distribute the weight of a rider evenly across the horse's back. If the saddle is made well and fits well, there is no need for anything thicker than a wool blanket between the horse and the saddle. This blanket acts as a barrier between the corrosive sweat of the horse and the leather of the saddle. Thicker pads, or blanket and pad combinations, can act as an aid to make a better fit between the horse and saddle, essentially filling in the relief of the horse's back. When doing this, the horseman is careful to use the least amount of blanket or pad that will work because of the risk of focusing weight and pressure on the horse's back by using too thick of a pad system.

All equipment and tack should be the very best that can be had, not the best that the horseman can afford. It is better to go without while saving money for the best than to waste money by buying an inferior product.

THE ENGAGEMENT OF AIDS

Pressure and Feel

> *If you can't explain it to a six-year-old, you don't understand it yourself.* (Albert Einstein)

> *Learning to easily explain helps you understand more full.* (Kelsay Stanton)

Pressure is a generic term used daily by horsemen. Pressure refers to both the mental stress, to learn and advance, that a horseman puts on a horse as well as the physical force a horseman exerts through the use of his aids. To engage any of the aids is to apply pressure.

The amount of physical or mental pressure a horse first encounters when learning is the amount of pressure the horse will always expect. Therefore, the horseman has the responsibility to exert enough physical pressure that the horse can clearly discern what is expected of him while at the same time produce an amount of mental pressure that will not scare the horse. The challenge in this comes from the horse's individuality. Since there is no standard within the vast array of individual horse personalities, the horseman must stay vigilant in his judgment. Some schools of thought suggest that the minimum amount of both physical and mental stress should be the foremost concern. When starting a horse, my foremost concern is a horse that has learned to learn. In my experience, working with minimum pressure as my goal only produces a horse that has learned to be confused.

The key to using pressure as a tool is in the knowledge that a horse learns from the release of pressure, not the pressure itself. No matter how much or how little pressure is used to create a reaction in a horse, the horse learns that he has reacted correctly to a horseman's desire when the pressure is released. The release of pressure before the horse has reacted in the desired manner will teach the horse an undesirable action while the maintaining of pressure after the horse has reacted properly will teach the horse nothing and will dull the horse in his acknowledgment of pressure and his desire to respond.

The engagement of the aids refers to anytime the horseman pulls on the bit or hackamore or uses the spurs, legs, seat, quirt, or bat to manipulate the horse's speed and direction. A horse is said to be light, soft, or supple when he reacts quickly and efficiently to the signal of the aids. In order to create a horse that is soft and supple, a horseman focuses his attentions on the release of pressure. The uses of soft/small pressure do not make a horse light! I was told as a boy, "Pull as hard as you please, but quit the instant the horse gives."

Feel

> *A beautiful woman looking at her image in the mirror may very well believe the image is herself. An ugly woman knows it is not.* (Simone Weil)

Feel is a term used by horsemen of all disciplines. The term "feel" has been highly mystified as a black-magic sixth sense that some have and some don't. This is false. Feel is nothing more than the active consciousness of one's body in regard to space and time and to other bodies moving through shared space and time. In other words, paying attention to how the bodies of both horse and rider are moving with regard to time and a given space. A horseman with a high degree of feel is one that has an active consciousness of his body and all its independent systems and movements. A horseman with feel keeps track of these independent body systems and their movements, exercising control over them in regard to the space they move through at any given time as well as the independent systems and movements of the horse regarding space and time and how the two (horseman and horse) affect each other. A horse with a high degree of feel does the same. Some horses and horsemen, through both nature and nurture, come by this consciousnesses easily. Feel can be taught to all, learned by all, and nurtured to a high degree by all; it only takes focus.

A Balanced Movement

When a horse moves on account of his natural tendencies, he moves without thought.

Pressure, release, and feel are the flagship theories of "natural horsemanship." The practices work very well in the beginning stages of a horse's career, however, depending on the horse's nature, falls short as the horse slowly advances into a finished horse and speed is added to the maneuvers. When working at higher speeds, a horseman can no longer depend on the horse's natural inclinations or innate tendencies to respond to external stimulation in a calculable manner. A horseman practicing art in his horsemanship depends on the balance of an athleticized horse to maneuver at speed. Pressure, release, and feel are used to foster this balance and athleticism in a young horse. As a horse advances, the horseman puts more stock into balance and the calculated execution of each footfall and less emphasis on the kind of intuition that many wrongfully regard as feel. When practicing natural horsemanship, the horseman attempts to change the way the horse moves by changing the way the horse thinks; a digest version of the theory would be that if the horse is happy and confident, then he will be willing to let a rider manipulate his movement. The theories of classical training dictate that if a horseman changes the way a horse moves, then he can change the way the horse thinks. Again, a digest version would be that if the horse moves with balance and collection, then he will be happy and confident. My personal experience leans toward the classical training method. The horse is all ego and learns about and perceives the world through movement. The horse can only be confident by himself when he moves with balance. The classical method of training is not only slower than natural horsemanship methods, it is also a lot more difficult practice because preying on the known inclinations of most all horses is far easier than actually athleticizing the horse. Both methods can and should be used and can be used hand in hand. It is far easier for a horseman to athleticize a horse if the horse already feels comfortable being around the horseman. Everything in moderation, including moderation. A horse can be started, trained, and finished using only classical training or both classical and natural horsemanship methods together; however, I have never seen a horse reach its full potential when the training strictly adhered to natural horsemanship.

TRUST

Trust is built with consistency.

—Lincoln Chafee

A horse does not have the capability to grasp an abstract idea like trust in the same manner that humans do. A horse expects that whatever happened previously in the society of men will happen again in the same manner. A horse's confidence in the horseman comes from the confidence of the horseman. It is very important to the horse to feel that he knows his place and the role he should play in a relationship. Whether the relationship be between one horse and another or many other horses or between horse and man, is not relevant to the horse's mind. A horse's confidence in the social structure he is engaged in, and the behavior that is expected of him, is what we humans refer to as trust. A horse has confidence that the way he has been treated and the way he has been expected to behave will be the same in all relationships with humans. Further, the horse expects that all humans will behave in a manner and uphold the social standard to which the horse is accustomed. Any deviation from the horse's expectations worries the horse and causes him to lose confidence (trust) in the human he is engaging. This is why a very gentle horse will often seem nervous when handled by a strange person. Through consistency and specific engagement that advises the horse how he is expected to behave, a horseman is able to gain a horse's trust. When the horse clearly understands the role he is to play in the relationship between himself and the horseman, he will play his role with supreme confidence. It depends on the horseman to show the horse what role is played by whom. Remember, dominance is not a character trait; it is an epiphenomenon, and the dominant role is played by whoever best understands what is going on in any given situation. When the horseman asserts that he/she understands the situation better than the horse, the horse will submit to the horseman. If the horseman consistently shows the horse that by submitting, the horse will be comfortable and can easily understand the situation, then the horse will "trust" the horseman.

When I was a boy, an old horseman told me, "Never trust a horse. They all kick, they all bite, and they all buck." As cynical as that sounds, it's true. The old-timer that spoke those words was not as gruff as he let on; what he meant by that harsh statement was, always trust every horse to be a horse, to behave like a horse, and to react to the things around him in the manner of a horse.

DECISION-MAKING

Quick decisions are unsafe decisions.

—Sophocles

When a horse makes a decision, it uses the combined knowledge of all past experiences to try and find similarities between what is happening and what has happened before. When a similarity is found and a connection is made between a new experience and a past experience, the horse has an indication as to the behavior that is expected of him. If the horse is unable to make a connection by observing similarities in an event with things that have happened in the past, the horse will revert to the instinctual urge to protect itself either through defense or retreat.

The horseman does not seek to make "friends" with the horse in his efforts to build confidence and trust in the horse because friendship is not necessary. The horseman seeks only to clearly indicate to the horse where the horse stands in the relationship and what behavior is expected of him. If the horse has submitted to the dominant personality of the horseman and has come to trust the judgment of the horseman, then the horse will make a decision of how to act based on the presence of the horseman. A horse does not know the difference between one scary situation and another. A funny shadow is the same as a tiger to the horse. A horse that has submitted to the judgment of the horseman will make a decision based on the proximity and judgment of the horseman. In other words, when faced with a scary situation, the horse will go through the catalog of memory in an effort to understand how to react or what decision to make. If the common denominator in good (or at least not scary) past decisions by the horse turns out to be the horseman and the judgment of the horseman, then the horse will confidently leave the decision in any situation up to the horseman and will act in accordance with the horseman's wishes. On the other hand, if the horse finds in the catalog of memory that the majority of decisions made that turned out to be bad or scary or harmful were dominated by the presence of the horseman, then the horse will decide to act on his own without regard to the wishes of the horseman. Horses make decisions based on what in the past has been comfortable and what has been uncomfortable and what those memories have in common with the present situation. A horseman strives to flood the memory of the horse with comfortable events that involve the presence or direction of the horseman. In this way, when faced with a decision, a horse will look to the direction of a horseman to indicate what decision will develop comfort for the horse.

Spooking

Terror made me cruel.

—Emily Bronte

When a horse spooks, he is attempting to flee from something that through experience with the thing, or more often than not, lack of experience with the thing makes the horse feel that the thing is dangerous. A horse will nearly always choose to flee from something that he feels is strange or dangerous if there is an opportunity to do so. To the horse, wisdom is the better part of valor, and it is far wiser to get away from something strange than to engage it. A horse that has confidence in his rider and the maneuvers that the rider sets him to, as well as confidence in the manner in which he has been taught to move, will not spook. Confidence of this kind comes from many hours of precise work with diligent attention paid to the release of pressure and the proper engagement of pressure. Building confidence in this manner takes timing, feel, and years of keen observation of horses.

Another method, while crude, is still very effective. This method is hyper-exposure with a stimulant of some kind. The stimulant can be a flag, plastic tarp, rope, or anything of a nature that a horse will want to move away from. The stimulant is engaged repeatedly in a manner that will induce the horse to move away. The engagement of the stimulant ceases when the horse shows tolerance of the object or action. This method is time-consuming and labor-intensive. The common assumption is that the horse relates the scary objects and situations to the flag that has been proven to be harmless. In fact, the time spent hyper-exposing a horse is simply an effort to show the horse his place and role in the relationship between horse and horseman and to expose the horse to the role the horseman intends to hold. Excellent timing of the engagement of pressure and the release of pressure as well as a high degree of feel are not paramount when practicing hyper-exposure methods because the nature of the method is not specific. The horseman is looking for tolerance of the action, not a specific reaction (movement). If the pressure is held after the horse has already committed to tolerance, no harm is done. Overuse of hyper-exposure can make a horse dull, so a horseman must be careful and use the method as a tool only when the practice of specific exercises are impossible because the horse is not gentle or has been mishandled or is defiant rather than submissive.

Horses have a tendency to spontaneously revert to their natural inclinations when they have been hyper-exposed to stimuli because stoically taking pressure without any release is not learning as much as becoming accustomed to discomfort. At some point, the horse will have been exposed to as much discomfort as he is mentally capable of withstanding and will lash out in fear or anger to protect himself from more discomfort. This is a "straw that broke the camel's back" situation, and the mental overload can be something very small and seemingly insignificant. One commonly hears people telling war stories about horse wrecks and some form of, "and for no reason at all, the horse…" when, in fact, there was a reason, and it may have been a small thing that set the horse off, but the reason was hyper-exposure that ruined the horse's confidence. A horse that has been started properly and submits to the horseman will not spontaneously revert. Hyper-exposure can be useful but must be used judiciously and be followed with proper training.

SUBMISSION

True strength lies in submission which permits one to dedicate his life, through devotion, to something beyond himself.

—Henry Miller

A submissive horse lends the use of his body and commits his physical and mental well-being to the horseman, thus submitting to the will of the rider. A defiant horse defies the will of the rider by securing the welfare of his physical and mental well-being to his own devices and reserving the use of his body to himself only. A horse that would rather bend to the will of his rider and continue to work regardless of strange things and actions is known to be submissive. A submissive horse will respond to the cues of the rider and not to outside influences. A defiant horse may allow himself to be ridden and may even perform some minor maneuvers, but will take control of the situation anytime he feels uncomfortable in any way.

Submission is different than trust in the sense that a defiant horse may trust wholeheartedly that a horseman cannot command him.

Horses have a natural tendency toward submission. While the dynamics of social hierarchy are vast within a horse herd, it is safe to say that all horses have played the role of submission in a submissive-dominant relationship, even if the horse has only been submissive to his dam.

Horses that have not yet reached full maturity (five years of age, generally speaking) are eager to grant submission even if the colt is dominant among his contemporaries. Further, all horses are willing to be submissive to some extent when they don't know what is going on or how to behave. In situations that render a horse unable to make a decision about how he should behave, he will show submission to any dominant personality that does know what is going on and is willing to show the horse how to behave. The horseman keeps this information in mind and never forgets that he (the horseman) is the only one between himself and the horse that does know what is going on in the starting process. The horseman also knows that when a horse is confused, he seeks information from a dominant individual; however, if no individual fills the role of dominance, the horse will assume he is the dominant individual and will treat all others as submissive (this includes humans). The dominant and submissive relationship is so deeply ingrained and so important to the horse, in his mind, every relationship must have a dominant individual, and the horse will shoulder the burden even if the role is one that he is uncomfortable with because someone must. It is the horseman's responsibility to be dominant, and if he shows dominance through action and body language (horses are experts at reading body language), the horse will willingly and gladly submit.

The horseman knows that a horse is a reactive animal and plans all engagement with the horse so that he (the horseman) creates all the action and pays close attention to never, if possible, allow situations that make him react to the horse's action. The horseman's goal with every engagement is to induce the horse to react to his actions. A horse is more likely to react than to create action; therefore, if a horseman finds himself in a position of reacting, he has caused a situation involving a series of reactions that he has little control over. At these times, the horseman's only course is to create a violent action that will jolt the horse into a controlled reaction. A violent action is risky for the horseman because the odds of a favorable reaction are low. Because of the risks in allowing the horse to create action, the horseman must carefully plan each step of his course. If he finds that he has misjudged the situation and the mentality of the horse, he quickly ceases all engagement and starts from a different point of course rather than risking reacting to the horse. The horseman has not failed if he steps back and begins again from a different point or from farther back. He fails only if the horse is able to gain control of the situation. By diligently and consistently planning his actions so that the horse will react to him, the horseman is able to quickly and firmly gain submission of the horse.

The Exercises Practiced in Gaining Submission

> *Tell me and I forget, teach me and I may remember,*
> *involve me and I learn.* (Benjamin Franklin)

The horseman gains a horse's submission by working the horse in incremental exercises; each exercise or "step," upon being mastered, opens the door for the next exercise. No single exercise is any more important than another; however, practicing the exercises in order is important. The first exercise is to teach the horse to properly move the feet. Once the horse has learned to move the feet properly, the horseman has gained control of where the horse goes and where it puts the body. At this stage, the young horse has only so much control of its own body placement. The three to five years of training that follow the starting of a colt will teach the horse body control.

A horse is moving its feet properly when it moves the hind feet first and steps forward, with the hind foot bringing it up and under the body. The horse should start all forward movement with the outside hindfoot (the foot opposite the direction of travel) engaging so that the horse is propelling itself with the hind feet. This shift of weight and propulsion with the hind feet is the beginning of collection. In turn, a horse should start all backward movement by shifting the inside hind foot back to hold the majority of the horse's weight.

The next exercise in gaining submission is creating independence in all four feet. Throughout the career of the horse, the horseman will continue to strive towed creating more independence in all the horses' body parts. In these steps in the training, the horseman holds the most elementary expectations. A horse that moves its feet independently moves them deliberately with an understanding of where that movement will place the body.

Finally, the horseman must develop a degree of flexibility in the horse's body so that the horse looks in the direction that it is traveling. The flexing of the head and neck with the independent propulsion of the feet are the beginning steps to a horse that moves straight.

Once a horse has become flexible in the head and neck and has an independent understanding of its feet and moves the feet properly, the horse will be confident of its own movement and of the role it plays in the relationship between itself and the horseman. A horse that is confident in the actions of a horseman and confident in the manner in which it is supposed to react to those actions will grant submission to the horseman. A submissive horse is a polite horse, and a polite horse is a gentle horse.

In all industry and all art, there is product and by-product. The duty of the artist is to make the by-product a valuable commodity. The by-product of music is an excess of sound, and the musician uses the extra sound to create resonance. The by-product of painting is an excess of brush strokes, and the painter uses the strokes to create depth. The by-product of working a horse is a horse that expects particular actions and reactions; the horseman uses the expectations to create a gentle horse.

The methods used for gaining submission in a horse by teaching it to properly move its feet, gain independence in all four feet, and develop flexibility are vast in variation. Every horseman has favored methods, as well as back-pocket methods that don't get used very often, and even secret methods that are passed down from master to apprentice. A specific method is only important in a given situation. It would be beyond the scope of this book to try to explain each method.

Theory in Practice

*In theory there is no difference between theory
and practice. In practice there is.*

—Yogi Berra

Up to this point, this book has been devoted entirely to theory. My original intentions were to write only about theory because each horse is different, and each horseman is different. Every horseman knows that a horse cannot be trained by theory alone (though my personal goal is to find enough understanding that I can train a horse by thought). Theory is a guideline for the work, and the work must be done to train a horse. The finest-trained horses in the world have been worked and worked and worked until they crave the work simply for the sake of work, and the finest horsemen in the world have worked even harder than any horse they have ever trained. Hard work alone also will not train a horse; there must be insight, understanding, confidence, passion, compassion, and practice.

The following chapter will be an account of how I start a colt from an un-halterbroke bronc to a started colt that has learned to learn and can start to train. In the practice of the art of horsemanship, I depend on thrift, precision, and efficiency. I strive constantly to boil everything I do down further and further so it is simpler for the horse to understand and less work for me. As time goes by, I find myself doing things more and more the way I was taught as a boy, the basic theory that one must get on a horse to start it and keep getting on the horse to finish it. I do not intend for the following chapter to be looked at as a how-to manual for starting colts; my intention is to show the marriage of ideas and practice and for the reader to see how a horseman designs his practices and sets up situations for a horse to learn. I would like the reader to look for the systematic steps taken so that each step lends itself to the next. The following chapter leaves out the hours and hours of work involved and distills the ideas behind the practices to the bare components of starting a colt.

An Unhaltered Bronc

A sailor buried on this shore
bids you set sail
for many a gallant bark, when I was lost
weathered the gale.

—A Greek anthology

Depending on where I am and the circles I am running in, an unhaltered bronc could be anything from a foal that is several days old to a five-year-old stallion. There is little difference in the actual practice of the work; the only difference is the level of precaution taken and the amount of pressure applied. The goal is the same and is based on the theory that a horse will always expect the same amount of pressure (signal) that it first encounters. In practice, this means that I make sure that I apply enough pressure from the start that the horse always expects that I can. Many people attempt to use the very least amount of pressure possible, thinking that this makes a horse soft, light, and responsive. I find that if the pressure is so imperceptible the horse must make a decision on what to do about it, the horse will quickly become dull to the pressure, and the horseman must "turn up the volume." If the volume is not turned up loud enough, then the horse becomes dull again, and soon an enormous amount of pressure is needed to even get the horse to notice. If the first pressure is enough that the horse has no doubt as to what is expected, less and less pressure can be used, and the horse becomes light and responsive because it always expects enough pressure. This applies to all pressure, not just haltering. In haltering a horse for the first time, I apply this theory. I prefer to halter colts either on weaning day or sometime before. The manner in which the horse is haltered (in a chute, by hand, from horseback) is not that important. I find that regardless of the first haltering method used, it takes ten or fifteen and sometimes twenty or thirty times of catching a colt before it is really good to catch. After the horse is haltered, my only objective is to show the horse that the halter and lead rope can stop the horse's movement. I keep in mind at this point that the horse is not pulling away from me; the horse is pushing against the halter pressure at the back of his head. We tend to think of horses as "away from pressure" animals, and in some regards they are; however, at close contact, when something or someone actually has a hold of them, a horse's first inclination is to push against that pressure. From the first haltering far into the training of a horse, I am striving to convince a horse to move away from the pressure instead of pushing back into it. The first several times that a horse is restrained by a halter are very important to me because a standard and history are set. Will the horse have a history of overcoming the pressure or of submitting to it? Knowing that the horse is pushing into the pressure and not pulling away from me, I do not try to halt the horse's motion by pulling harder than he. Instead, I simply hold the pressure and allow the horse to push as much as he wants. Within a few minutes, the horse will realize that he is pushing against a force that cannot be pushed away and will stop. I do not try to get the horse to move away from the pressure by taking a step forward; it is enough for now that the horse has stopped. After the horse has stopped, I create movement in the horse by stepping into the horse's personal space. When the horse moves away from me (as he should), I apply pressure on the halter by creating a situation where the horse will move into pressure and hold it until the horse stops pushing against the halter. I do this from a variety of angles until I can stop the horse's movement from any point in front of its shoulder. This exercise is very efficient because it teaches the horse to move away from the pressure I create with my body in a precise direction, to stop movement when pressure is applied by the halter (the beginning of giving to pressure), and within a few minutes, this breaks down the horse's personal bubble to a point that I can touch the horse. With a few applications of this, the horse can be safely tied solid. As stated before, I prefer to do this work when the horse is a weanling. After the horse shows clearly that it will cease movement when the pressure from the halter is applied, I turn them out to be horses until they are long yearling. The timeline and the age of the horse is not important, though, and the steps can be followed without a break. This is to say that one can halter break a three-year-old colt and continue through the starting processes without a break in the timeline.

LEADING

We call a halter broke horse "broke to lead" when, in fact, the horse has learned to give and move away from the pressure at the back of its head and follows the individual that controls the pressure. When leading a horse, the biggest mistake a person can make is trying to pull a horse. Even if the horse is very small, it likely cannot be pulled forcefully by a human. I also keep in mind that if I pull, I am in a tug of war with a horse, and he has the strongest part of his body (the neck) to "tug" with. At this stage in the training, I start working toward submission from the horse by practicing the exercises discussed in previous chapters. I must set the horse up to respond to my actions in the way I desire by making the reaction he gives seem like the only possible reaction he can give. I create the movement by moving toward the horse's hip, or at least behind his shoulder, while holding the lead rope and flexing the horse's neck in an arch (this can be done with a flag, etc. I do the work from the back of another horse). Both the horse and I know that I can stop the forward movement with the halter, so the only option the horse has to preserve his personal space is to step his inside hind foot forward and under his body, crossing the forward line of travel of the other foot. I have now compelled the horse to do a forehand turn. I have started teaching the horse to properly move the hind feet and have broken ground on the concepts of independence in the body and flexibility. At no point in this exercise am I concerned with the horse "leading" forward or being gentle; both of those concepts are by-product of the work. If the work is done correctly, the by-product will, without a doubt, be present. I do this exercise both directions, and in a very few minutes the horse is stepping forward with all four feet and following me around in larger and larger circles and then in straight lines and figure eights. The exercise is complete when the horse moves its hips away and its body forward from the propulsion of the hind feet with any change in my direction.

Very often in horsemanship, the horseman is working toward the by-product of his work, so what is going on can be the opposite of what it looks like. This is the case with leading the horse. Distilled down, leading is not so much an effort to get the horse from point A to point B as much as it is an effort to get a horse to leave point A. Distilled even further, and the main objective to leading a horse is keeping the horse from going where the horseman does not want the horse to be. Getting the horse to where the horseman does want the horse to be is the by-product. I don't mean to paint this in a negative light, but I find things easier to understand myself and easier to teach the horse if I distill a concept down to its simplest form. In order to get a horse to go with me, I must keep him from going other places. Based on this simple idea, I use the lead to stop the horse from going places rather than using it to convince the horse to follow me. If the direction I am going is the only place I don't stop him from going, or the only place I allow him to go, the horse will soon start to follow me.

An old friend used to say, "I don't bother with leading till I get a horse good and broke. May as well get the easy part done first and see if the nag is worth all the effort of teaching him to lead." The joke here is that it is really a long time before the horseman is able to lead the horse well; the horse may follow well, but it is mostly be stopped from going anywhere other than where the horseman is going. I find this concept a lot easier to grasp and a lot more consistent than abstract ideas like feel and timing. Much of what I will be doing throughout the starting process will be based on the idea of distilling a concept down to the simplest form and working toward the by-product of my work.

Like all art forms the by-product of the work creates the depth.

HOBBLES

Next, I exercise the concept of independence in the horse's limbs. Remember, at this stage, all work is on concept. These exercises are the foundation for all the same exercises I will do for the rest of the horse's life and are a direct precursor to the actual riding of the colt when I am concerned with go, stop, and turn. To start my work on the independence of the horse's limbs, I hobble the horse's front feet. I suppose that there could be some controversy about the practice of hobbling; however, that is for another book. Let it be stated that I have hobbled thousands of horses; many of which had a breeding fee that was well over my yearly income. It is a safe and valuable practice. If, however, the reader is a die-hard anti-hobbling believer, the same work can be done without hobbles. It just takes longer. To prepare a horse to be hobbled, I use the end of my lead rope. I stand shoulder to shoulder with the horse, facing the tail. By this stage, the horse is accustomed to me being in direct contact with his body at the point of his shoulder because all my previous work of moving his hips have accustomed him to it. Each exercise should prepare the horse for the next exercise. I have planned it this way because this is the safest place for me to be. Most horses cannot cow-kick me from here, cannot strike me, and cannot bite me without moving into me. If he attempts any of these foul practices, the horse must move into me, essentially pushing me away to a safe distance. The horse learned to move his hips away from me in the previous exercise, so when he moves, I will still be in a safe proximity from the horse. Many styles of preparatory work on a young horse teach the horse to come to the horseman when frightened or uncomfortable. I find this to be dangerous because even a horse that intends no harm is enough larger than me to do great harm if he runs into me. If a horse gets scared or uncomfortable, I want him to move away from me. This will be important later. In the starting process, I never attempt to hinder a horse that is moving away from something it doesn't like. Again, this theory builds on itself as I later compel the horse to move away from and then give to pressure of all kinds. Much of the preparatory work that follows has been termed "desensitizing," and I could not disagree more with this concept. I am in no way attempting to desensitize anything. In fact, I am striving to make the horse more sensitive in everything I do. To be advised by one of the five senses, analyze the sensation and react to it according to past experiences, is to be more sensitive. This is what I want from the horse. To be advised by one of the five senses and ignore the sensation completely is what I don't want. The "desensitize camp" works toward acceptance of a foreign sensation; I work toward tolerance of a foreign sensation. Again, this work toward tolerance will pay off later when I saddle and ride the horse. To prepare the horse to be hobbled, I flick the end of the lead rope around the horses' front legs until the horse tolerates the sensation. I don't care if the horse moves away or does not like the sensation. I care only that he comes to tolerate the sensation. If I have done the rest of my work correctly, I should move to making the same motion and sensation with a pair of hobbles within a few minutes and have the horse hobbled in a few more. Once the horse is hobbled the first time, I must be prepared to assist the horse by using my halter and lead rope to stop him. The horse's first impulse will be to panic and to run; of course, he can't run because he's hobbled, so he will lunge. Every time the horse lunges forward, I apply pressure on the halter from a position behind the point of the shoulder to stop forward movement. This is an angle akin to the angle I will be applying pressure from in the next step and later in the first ride. The angle is calculated so that when I am on the horse, and the effect of the pull matters the most, I will have already taught the horse to give to a similar pull. Without knowing it, the horse is shifting its weight to the hind feet to lunge forward and further developing collection. Also, by applying pressure on the halter from an angle behind the point of the shoulder, I am building the framework for flexibility in the neck. Most horses will make three to five lunges before stopping.

At this point, I stand shoulder to shoulder with the horse just as I did when preparing the horse for hobbles and soothe the horse. I like to brush the mane and caress the neck, producing a valuable by-product for later. I start from the shoulder and work my way toward the hips, running my hands across the horse's body. The horse will move the hips away from me, furthering the correct movement of the hind feet and introducing the independent movement of all four feet. I brush the tail, for no other reason than I need to do something once I get there. Most horses will stand still and flex the neck to watch me after a few rotations; however, this is not necessarily the goal; the independent action of the hind feet is the goal.

Before I go on, I introduce the horse to the moral, or feed bag. I grain all my horses with a moral for several reasons. First, it gives the horse a chance to eat with its head down as nature intends, stretching the longissimus dorsi that runs most of the length of the body and is the strongest muscle in the body. Second, the moral insures far less waste than graining in a tub or bucket; and finally, because it makes a horse good to catch and good about having his head handled. For health reasons, I don't like to grain young horses. A cup of oats or sweet feed is enough to make them come up and want to be caught and not enough to affect the horse's skeletal growth. I put the moral on first while the horse is hobbled because one in one hundred will get claustrophobic, having the moral over the nose, and throw a wall-eyed fit without even noticing the grain. After the horse has finished throwing a fit, they tend to notice the grain and eat it and never have an issue again. I put the moral on the first time while hobbled to prevent the horse from striking. Of well over a thousand horses I have fed with a moral, I recall only two that I needed to hobble for several days in a row to feed with the moral. In truth, this practice is like living in a houseboat and keeping flood insurance, but it's better than getting in a wreck.

ROMPER EL CABALLO

Once I am satisfied with the independent action of the hind feet, I must introduce the independent action to the front feet. I unhobble the horse and make my way back to the horse's hip, holding on to the lead rope. The horse by this point is comfortable with my presence behind the point of the shoulder. Once at the hip, I grasp the horse's tail with my off hand and continue to hold the lead. I hold a tension that the horse is comfortable with, and when the horse finds balance, I tie the lead rope to the tail. From this point, I can gradually increase the amount of flexion that I ask from the horse's neck. This increase in flexion is aimed at creating movement from the horse. With every incremental increase of flexion, the horse will first move the hips away from me in the independent manner that it has been shown; however, when the pressure is not released, the horse will search for a new answer. In a few moments, the horse will shift its weight to the hind feet and move the front feet independently forward and toward me. Again, every exercise prepares the horse for the next exercise, and preparation by me is taken so that what I want from the horse seems to him to be the only thing that can be done. By the time the horse moves the front feet with some degree of independence, the horse has had sufficient introduction to flexing the neck. My last exercise is to apply pressure on the halter, starting at a roughly forty-five-degree angle standing at the point of the horse's shoulder. The pressure is released when the horse flexes the neck far enough to put slack in the lead rope. The horse will attempt to move hind or forefeet along with flexing the neck but will soon find that independent movement of the neck is all that is asked and will stand firm and flex. I move back toward the hip in small increments until the horse flexes the neck from applied pressure that comes from approximately the same angle that I will be applying pressure from when mounted. Keep in mind that all exercises are done to the same degree from both sides of the horse because there is a horse in the right eye and a horse in the left, and you can't expect the horse in the left eye to tell the one in the right eye that you are coming.

I do not ask for perfection in any of these exercises. I ask only for tolerance and a clear understanding of what is being asked. Perfection is not necessary. I seek only for a marked improvement from the previous work. This search for marked improvement will be the cornerstone of the training process from this point on. If I can advance a horse a little, I stop before I wreck something that I will need to fix later. While working a young horse, I often think of what Ezra Pound said, "You cannot get out of hell in a hurry. Let us remain here as long as possible just to fool the demons."

The practice of tying the head to the tail and compelling the horse to move around himself is as old as any practice in horseman-ship. The man I learned it from called it *romper el caballo*, literally, "break the horse." The meaning was to break the horse out of his tracks and compel the horse to bend or break at particular joints in the neck and back. Anymore I will not get on a horse that has not been "broke" in this manner. I find the exercise to be invaluable, and I continue the practice in degree throughout the career of the horse. At any point in a training ride, if I am called away, I will tie the horse's head to his tail while I attend to whatever chore for which I was needed. Further, if a horse has been turned out for a season on break, I find that tying to the tail is a quick and easy way to limber the horse before starting back to work. By teaching the horse this exercise early in the training process, I save myself and the horse later down the road.

When I put the first ride on the horse, the tail-tying practice will pay dividends. Very often when the horse feels the weight of a rider for the first time, the horse will stiffen its body as a response to the change in balance. The longissimus dorsi that I have men-tioned several times earlier will stiffen the neck and body. Because this and other muscles are tight, instead of relaxed, the horse will be retarding his ability to move with his own strength. The first step of the first ride is the hardest part of the whole process because of the horse being tight. Getting the horse to quietly, and confidently, take the first step is difficult because the horse feels like he cannot take a step because of the tension in his body. As a result, the horse often plunges into the first moment, and the result is a wall-eyed horse fit. If I have already trained the horse to give to a pull by tying to the tail, I can flex the neck, relax the body, and create an opportunity for the horse to step off quietly.

HOBBLING THE HIND FEET

When the horse is comfortable being tied to its tail, I take to preparing the hind legs for the next step in the process. Just as I prepared the front feet for hobbles, I prepare the hind feet by flicking the tail of a rope around the hind legs until the horse is tolerant of the action and feel. It is not imperative to use a rope, as anything will do; often I use my jacket or anything else I put my hands on. Again, I mean the literal feel of the rope touching the hind leg and not the metaphorical feel. I do this with the horse's head tied around not because he cannot kick me but because it is very difficult for the horse to kick at me from this position, and most will only ever try once. When I am confident that the horse will tolerate the hind feet being handled, I hobble the hind feet, untie the tail, and use the halter and lead rope to help the horse in the same way that I helped the horse when the front feet were hobbled. Hobbling a horse's front and hind feet will pay dividends later when the farrier handles the feet and will also prevent a wreck if and when the horse ever gets tangled up in a rope or wire. They will not kick and cut themselves; they will submit. With the hind feet hobbled, I take a gunny sack and rub the horse all over. Anything will do, but the scratch of a gunny sack feels good to a horse. Anytime I can I try to make things pleasing to the horse, I rub the sack up and down all four legs inside and out, under the belly and flank, between the legs, around the neck, and all over the head and back. In about fifteen minutes, the horse will submit to the stimulus of touch all over the body. The horse may not like it, but I am not concerned with that. I look only for tolerance and submission. As it is, most horses do like this part and often close the eyes and sigh happily. At this point, I am prepared to saddle the horse.

SADDLING

The horseman sees his saddle as the sailor sees his ship. It is the wind that gets him across the ocean, but the ship gets him there with dry feet.

The first saddling for a colt can either be a frightening and stressful ordeal or a simple transition that makes perfect sense to the young horse. If the horseman has done a proper job of building confidence in the young horse and has used the time needed, then there should be no reason that this step in the process should be anything more than another stimulating exercise for the horse.

I start by hobbling the horse. By this stage, the horse is very familiar with being hobbled and understands that the hobbles retard forward movement. Once the horse has been hobbled, I put on the blanket (the use and fit of blankets pads and saddles has been discussed). If the horse shows any degree of intolerance to the blanket, I spend the time needed to regain that tolerance. When the saddle is put on the first time, as well as every other time throughout the horse's career, a horseman must be mindful of his manners. A horseman must be mannerly and respectful of the horse if he is to expect the horse to be mannerly and respectful. Being mannerly when saddling the horse means setting the saddle on the horse's back instead of throwing or dropping the saddle on the horse. It is also important that the stirrups and rigging of the saddle do not bang against the horse or become tangled under the saddle, between it and the horse's back. I walk around the horse to drop the cinch for the first several saddlings to give the horse another chance to see me out of the other eye. Thrift in movement and forethought are of the utmost importance at this point. Before I swing the saddle onto the horse's back, I lean slightly into the horse. I know that the horse will lean into me slightly because he is an "into pressure" animal. In this way, I have further retarded forward motion because it is harder for the horse to move if he is leaning; plus I have set myself up to be safe because if the horse does lunge, he will push me away to a safe distance. Having me to lean on slightly gives the horse a feeling of confidence. In days to come, I will demand that the horse stand alone to be saddled, but for the first few times, I am willing to do a little extra for him so that later he will be willing to do a little extra for me.

Cinching the Saddle

The horse should be tolerant of being touched in the girth area before the first saddling. When I go to cinch the horse for the first time, I take a moment to reiterate that tolerance by running the back of my hand across the girth area a few times. I always use the back of my hand when touching a horse on sensitive parts of the body such as the girth or flank; the horse is less sensitive to the back of the hand than the palm and fingers. I don't really know why and have not found any reason through research. I do know that I have handled a lot of horses, and they most all seem less irritated by the feel of the back of my hand than by the feel of my palm and fingers. At one time in my life, I would not have cared about the why; however, at this stage of my life, the question nags me. When I was a boy, I observed a very gruff and violent old man soothe a very scared horse by rubbing it with the back of his hand and the hair side of his forearm. I have done the same ever since.

It is important for the comfort of the horse that the center bar of the cinch lays across the center of the horse's sternum. This should be checked and adjusted to fit before cinching the horse. When I start to tighten the cinch, I expect the young horse to lean against me slightly and position myself to accommodate this. This is one of the few times I ever allow a horse to encroach on my personal space; I allow it for the first several saddlings because it offers some comfort and confidence to the young horse. When a horse is nervous, he will squeeze in against his companions. This is simple herd psychology, and a horseman can judge just how nervous or confident a young horse is about being cinched the first time by gauging how hard the horse leans. Most horses are claustrophobic to some degree, so this nervousness is perfectly normal. I snug and loose the cinch several times until the horse ceases leaning on me. I keep in mind that the cinch needs only to be tight enough to keep the saddle on. For the first several saddlings, I use a very thin blanket and use a saddle that fits (as well as a saddle can fit the immature shape of a young horse) to facilitate the saddle staying on with a snug cinch. I do not, however, allow the cinch to be too loose. A horse that is cinched tight enough from the beginning will soon lose any "cinchiness" while a horse that is allowed to move on a loose cinch will learn to bind up on a tighter cinch. This is very important because once a horse starts to cinch bind, they really never stop. Very few habits are as dangerous as a cinch binder.

Cinching the horse should be done in the most efficient manner possible so the horse can be unhobbled and allowed to feel the saddle and cinch with full liberty in his feet. If the horse stands hobbled and cinched for too long, a risk is run that the horse will become bound up and claustrophobic. This leads to cinch binding and other undesirable habits. This is to say that speed and efficiency are of the utmost importance at this stage; however, one should avoid rushing. Nothing in life is done well if it is rushed. Some of these simple and seemingly small parts of the process are exactly what can spoil a horse and are the reasons I suggest all horses should be started for at least ten rides by a professional.

I like to let the horse move off several strides on his own before I ask him off. I desire the horse to move off softly and quietly and do everything in my power to direct the horse in that manner. A lot of times a horse will stand quietly saddled for some time before moving off on his own. As a kid, this time would have been a prime opportunity for me to offer a smoke to whichever old man happened to be using me as a test dummy. While we waited for the colt to step off, he would spin me a tale of lost youth. Anymore, I generally pour myself a cup of coffee and think back to those times; sometimes I can mine a little forgotten knowledge. Once the horse is moving off, it is perfectly normal for him to grab, gain speed, and get crooked in his body. A horse's only method of defiance to a rider or saddle is to speed up and get crooked in his body. Some call this bucking, but it is nothing more than gaining speed and getting crooked. The vast majority of horses will do this to varying degrees for the first few saddlings because the saddle changes the horse's weight and balance. When an untrained horse loses balance, he will always speed up and try to "outrun" the loss of balance. When this doesn't work, he will contort his body in an effort to find a way of moving that suits the new balance. I move the horse back and forth between the three gaits in one direction until the horse has found balance and a regulated stride. It is important to keep the horse moving until he travels with his body straight and does not lean toward the inside or outside his movement. In a few minutes, I will be on the horse, and any leaning will be extenuated by my height and weight, thus throwing the horse further off balance. Once the horse is moving correctly around the pen in one direction, I halt the horse and let him find balance and stride going the other direction. I do not roll the horse back and forth, changing directions, unless he absolutely cannot find his balance. I am satisfied with slowly allowing the horse to find his balance and stride if he will. By rolling the horse back and forth in direction, I stimulate him to react to me and my movement rather than learn how to carry the weight of the saddle. I already know how the horse will react to my movement, and doing this does nothing to advance the horse unless he absolutely cannot or will not find balance on his hind legs and regulated stride by going forward. If I feel that I must roll him back a few times to help him find balance, I will do so, and then disengage pressure so that he will learn to balance from the release.

I can tell that the horse has found balance under the weight of the saddle when he is moving in a manner that arches his body from his poll to his tailhead at the same angle as his line of travel. So if he is traveling in a sixty-foot circle, I want his body arched to the same degree as the circle. A sixty-foot circle is really as small as I can expect the horse to be able to move in correctly for any extended period of time. Smaller enclosures inhibit the horse's movement to a degree that finding balance is very difficult for the average horse.

This, of course, is not measured with a caliper and compass but with experience and empathy for the athletic abilities and limitations of the individual.

This process can be done in its entirety in one setting or in several or one step per day or on step for several days until the horse works with a marked improvement. Each horse is an individual, and each horse will be different. An experienced horseman will be able to tell, with a high degree of accuracy, when the horse is learning and when the horse is simply reacting. This takes years of keen observation. Some horses need short breaks between steps. Others benefit from longer breaks. Some need no break at all. The key to success is not knowing what to do, or even how; the key is knowing when.

MOUNTING

Now my turn for thin ice and tigers.

—Ezra Pound

Once the horse has found a degree of balance (I say *a degree* because I will spend the majority of my time over the horse's career attempting to further his balance), it is time to get on and ride. I like to give the horse several minutes to catch his breath and slow his heartbeat before proceeding, and if the horse seems played out from the experience of the first saddling, I put him away and begin again tomorrow. An ever-present credo in my mind when working with any horse is "mañana." This is a simple way of saying, "I haven't messed up anything I can't fix yet, so I'll start again tomorrow." I think of this before any new advancement of the young horse.

Los tres pasos de muerte (the three passes of death)—as a boy I learned this maneuver by this name.

Before mounting, I tighten my cinch, then I take the rein of my hackamore (this goes for snaffles and halters as well) and place it behind the cantle board of my saddle opposite the side I am standing, and turn the horse around to face me. This does several things for me and the horse. First, it allows the horse to move off in a controlled manner after the cinch has been tightened. Second, I am able to simulate the pull and direction I will be using once on his back; and third, it gives the horse an opportunity to "switch eyes." When practicing this action, the horse sees me from the left eye first. When he follows the pull, he can no longer see me out of either eye for a moment, and then upon completion of the maneuver, he again sees me, but out of the right eye. This switching of eyes is very hard for a horse to understand. When I am on the horse, he will be able to see me out of both eyes but will also be switching eyes as we maneuver. I practice this on both sides until the horse does the work efficiently and is not bothered by the switch. I keep this exercise up for a long time, at least the first thirty rides or so. It gives the horse confidence and starts the horse into a habit of collecting himself (shifting his balance to his hind legs) before any lateral movement. I strive to direct my own actions and the actions of the horse to make the work easier for the horse to understand and to lay a foundation for work in the future so that when I advance the horse to more and more complicated maneuvers and ask for greater athleticism, I will have a base for the horse to work from and a means of simplifying the maneuver for the horse.

Next, I back the horse for several strides. By this time, I have backed him from the ground often, but never with a saddle on his back. Also, I will ask him to back at least one stride before I end the first ride, so I would like the cue to be fresh in his mind.

A horse is strong, but a young horse is not strong enough to stand still while I mount unless his feet are placed directly under his body with a wide stance. Backing a horse a few strides will almost always set his feet correctly. I want his left front foot slightly ahead of the right and set wider from his body and his right hind under his barrel. Positioning the feet in this way gives the horse a solid stance and gives me an advantage for mounting the first time. The majority of my weight while mounting will be held by the horse's left front limb. I cheek a horse to mount (take hold of the headstall with my left hand and bend the horse slightly to the left), so the combination of my weight on the leg with the wider stance and the arch to the left in his neck makes it harder for the horse to move off while I am mounting. It also gives me an advantage in the way I can balance and manipulate my weight to assist the horse. Once up, I will turn the horse's head to the right to be sure he has seen me on both sides of him. If the horse is still confident at this point, I will ask him to take his first steps toward being broke. I ask him to move off for the first time to the right where I have already positioned his right hind leg to bear the weight and balance changes that have occurred. Again, I have done everything in my power to direct the process so that the horse will learn to be balanced and collected under my weight. By thinking ahead and planning my actions, I can make every advancement and maneuver easier for the horse.

THE FIRST RIDE

It doesn't matter if it's the first time a horse carries a rider, as long as it's not the first time the rider has sat a horse.

Some years ago, a young trainer asked me, "What is the best colt you ever started?"

I responded, "The one I start tomorrow."

I want the first ride for a horse to be the easiest and simplest part of the day. I ask for very little, only that the horse goes, stops, and turns. Depending on the age and maturity level of the horse, I may allow the horse to break from a walk to other gaits; however, I generally try to keep the horse at a walk. Balance and stride must be found at the walk before it can be found in the other gaits, so I see no reason to do anything other than walk until an advancement in the horse's balance and stride is made at the walk. This is not a hard-and-fast rule for me. If it comes down to breaking into another gait or getting in a fight to maintain the walk, I will let the horse break. When the horse finds a degree of balance and a consistent stride at the walk, I stop the horse, turn the horse, and go the other direction. This has already been a big day for the horse, so once I have gone both directions and stopped and turned both directions, I will stop the horse, back him at least one stride, and put him away.

One of the most difficult parts of starting a horse is continuing to do things in the proper order and resisting the urge to jump ahead. A horseman can get into serious trouble and promote undesirable traits in a horse that take a long time to fix if he depends on feel and guesswork about a horse. Many horses feel like they can be advanced very quickly from this stage, and some horsemen allow and encourage the horse to jump ahead. At this stage, if I were to start right in loping circles and advancing lateral and longitudinal flex-ion, I would be skipping the lessons of learning to balance correctly with the weight of the rider. The horse may be able to perform more advanced maneuvers because he is athletically superior; however, I would still need to go back and teach the rudimentary lessons later on. Complicating the learning by skipping ahead and going back is inefficient and wasteful, plus the horseman runs a huge risk of confusing the horse or forgetting a step that was skipped. In the best scenario, the horseman wastes time; and in the worst scenario, the horse is spoiled. For me, the risk is not worth the reward, and I think it is better to progress slowly than to skip and come back.

As a child, I was taught a rather-complicated riff on the guitar before I was taught the basic notes and chords. As an adult, I can still play the complicated piece but have yet to master the basic chords. I try to remind myself of this when I start a very talented colt. I wish I could say I learned this from one of the old men of my youth, but I would be lying. I learned this the hard way, and unfortunately, I am a slow learner, and the lesson took several ruined horses to stick.

The next several rides will be more of the same. I don't attempt to advance a horse until he allows me to use my aids to put him into balance and hold him there for a few strides and start in any direc-tion with the initial movement coming from the hind legs. When the horse allows me to manipulate his body while riding him, he has grasped the concepts of balancing with the weight of a rider and has shown me that he has learned the process of learning. For the next three years, I will slowly advance him in his stride, speed, balance, athleticism, and confidence by systematically refining his movement, building his strength, and shifting his center of balance. This is a started colt.

METAMORPHOSIS

*The only way to learn is to mess something up
and try to figure out how to fix it.*

—Bill Arthur

*You won't live long enough to make all the mistakes
you need to learn from, so pay close attention to
other people's mistakes and learn from them.*

—Elliot Seagle

As I stated before, I was hesitant to write about my own methods. I can see the ideas being misunderstood and misused or misjudged because of the lack of understanding that I have about writing. As it were, I wrote myself into a corner and had no choice.

My own work with horses is in a constant metamorphosis. I changed some small things in my method while I was writing, I changed a little more while I was editing, and I shall probably change a little more tomorrow or the next day. This is how art works. Each of us must be in vigilant search for better, more efficient ways of working. I try a little something here and get no result, so I abandon the idea. I try something else here that I heard from a friend and see some promise, so I try a little more. A thing may come to fruition, and it may not. It doesn't matter. Some of the things I have learned about horses I am pleased with; other things I wish I could have learned not to do from others. Every day we struggle, and that is all that can be done. I have been asked if, under different circumstances, would I go about my work in another manner with a different method? I am sure I would, but I cannot say what the difference would be. Each horse is different. From time to time I fall back on methods that I don't normally use and don't particularly care for, but I do it because I think the method will work. The *Book of the Five Rings* by Musashi sums up the idea that all methods have advantages over others, and all methods have disadvantages under others. Victory is Musashi's goal, and a confident, balanced colt is mine. I will do anything necessary to reach my goal.

All horses are the same to me. Horses I have started have competed in every major futurity and derby in America. I am proud of them. Horses I have started have carried cowboys through their day-to-day work and trail riders across the country and 4-H riders through weekend playdays. I am proud of them as well. If I could track all the horses that have been under my saddle, I think I could find them in every part of the industry around the world, and I am proud of them all. In the end, the horseman must treat futurity hopefuls, Kentucky Derby prospects, ranch horses, backyard projects, and eight-year-old BLM stallions the same—with respect. Each one is entitled to the same things that we are: life, liberty, and the pursuit of happiness.

PREFIX

I didn't intend for this. I didn't intend for any of this. This is not my life's work but rather a series of events that I have had little control over. I never meant to train horses for a living. I meant to do as little work as possible until I was not able to work at all and then move to a Mexican beach and think my remaining years away. It seems, though, that, as humans, we have less control over our own lives and our own passions than the sages and philosophers led us to believe.

I started riding horses for pay when I was very young because I come from a people that say, "One must earn one's own way," and riding didn't seem like work. I kept up the habit because, at a certain point, I came to the realization that I didn't know how to do anything else. I have always intended that someday, when I had a little to my name, a good saddle or two and a few good bits, and possibly a nice horse to ride, I would go home and take a job on a ranch somewhere and live quietly, taking care of cattle, and never go to town again. I don't think this will ever happen.

I started this book in a fit of rage about ten years ago. A young heir to a ranching dynasty allowed that, through no fault of his own, he didn't really understand how a snaffle bit works. I wasn't angry with him, but instead I was angry that the young man didn't know, and he of all people had every opportunity to learn. This book started as a few notes of things I wanted to tell him, jotted down in a dentist's office in Pryor, Oklahoma. What I thought would be a handful of talking points filled a small notebook while I waited for my better half, who was getting her wisdom teeth pulled. It seems that knowledge begets knowledge, and when seven or eight notebooks were filled with ideas and questions and arguments to my own ideas, I knew I had a problem. I started consolidating the information into larger notebooks, some books of truths that I held to be self-evident, others of questions, and still others of things that I knew to be false. Over the next few years, the words spilled out of their pages, and the things that I knew were fact and the things that I knew were fiction started to meld together. At no other point in my life has my ability and knowledge as a horseman grown with such unmarked precedence, nor have I enjoyed the work so much as the last few years when I really started to learn.

By the time I had all my thoughts in order, the young man that had started it all no longer cared. He had lost his interest in horses and saw them only as a tool that must be used to take care of cattle and to make money. This disheartening fact led me to desire to write a book in the hopes that perhaps another like him would not learn to see a horse as a slave but as a canvas.

I didn't know how to write a book, and my efforts were mired by my own ignorance. It's not that I didn't try hard; it's that I didn't try hard in the correct place. I repeatedly started in the middle and worked both directions, attempting to herd the words into some kind of order. Sifting through my own notes, I saw a scribble a quote from a man I spoke to years ago.

"How do you start a colt?"

"Get on him and ride."

"How do you finish a horse?"

"Keep getting on him and keep riding."

I realized that I had been doing exactly the things I warned against in my own notes, skipping ahead and going back and forth, trying to make it all fit rather than starting at the beginning and stopping at the end. The work was effortless after that; the words came and were set down and made sense to me.

The work is much shorter than I envisioned it to be. There are hundreds of handwritten pages that have been distilled and cropped and hedged to be this work. I am a firm believer in frugality both in life and in art, and left to my own whims, I would cut the words back and back until the whole work was the two sentences that the old man told me, "Get on him and ride. Keep getting on and keep riding."

I make my living off of a horse's back. The food on my children's plate and the roof over their heads were paid for in horse sweat, and I see no reason why that will change in my lifetime. My sincerest wish is that a single reader finds inspiration in these words and chooses to see horsemanship as an art. In our modern world, horses are a hobby and not the necessity they once were. If a single person reads this book and chooses horses over tennis, I will feel that I have given the horse what he has given me.

Thank you.

CONCLUSION

There is no definition to a started horse. There is no set number of rides or work that clearly defines when the starting ends and the training begins. Some years ago, I called a horse started the first time my butt hit the saddle, and I was training with the first step. Nowadays I call one started when he lets me hold the body straight while in motion, and then the training begins. In another ten years, who knows? I have a horse that was flunked out of several other programs as a two-year-old because he bucked so hard under saddle no one ever risked stepping on to him. He is eleven now, and I will have him all his life because it would take six months to write the owner's manual for what he will and will not stand for; yet my two-year-old daughter rides him all over, and he never indulges in his pet idiosyncrasies. The horse frustrates me at times because, as trained as he is, I cannot always depend on him to act like a citizen. At the end of the road in our knowledge is a gate marked "frustration," and I lack the knowledge. My little girl can train him though, and I sometimes wonder, did I start him and train him, or did I just spend all those years starting him so she could train him?

I asked my older sister to edit this work because she is a professor, and I am not. She is not an English professor, but she has several college degrees, and I went to college several days in a row before I spit the bit on formal education. Some of her little notes asked, "Why did you put a semicolon here?" and I had to giggle to myself because I didn't really know. I don't really know what semicolons do. The other reason I asked her to edit is because she is the kind of person I wrote this work for—a professional person that has some knowledge about horses and horsemanship but no closet intention of becoming a horse trainer. I figured if the work made sense to her, then it would make sense to others as well. Of course, it makes perfect sense to me. I wrote it.

Besides being a college professor, my sister is a scientist and has been published in several peer-review journals. Scientists are big on citing their information. I am not. Over the phone she told me that I needed to cite my work because I mentioned specific theories without properly explaining what the theory was as well as using certain uncommon scientific words as if everyone already knew the definition. "I had to do some research to really understand what you were talking about," she said. I replied, "You pass." The entire work is about learning to learn, and my intention was to write in a manner that would cause people to go look things up and discover more through learning, just like I learned to learn and just as I teach a horse to learn. Learning is exponential, and every day of a horseman's life is a pass or fail course, so I wrote with that spirit.

Every draft of this work I have had to soften and add voice. The first draft was pleasing to me but read like the book of numbers in the King James version of the Bible. I am certain that no other human would have cared for it. I write about starting colts in a cold monotone because I think about starting colts in cold monotone. I am cold about the work because the work is my job, not my hobby. I can promise that in my own hobby, I am as giddy as any preteen horse-crazy girl. I owe the longevity of my career starting colts to this coolness. Not only has it kept me safe, it has kept me sane. There have been many before me, most of them more talented, that have fallen in love with every horse they worked and had their heart broken beyond repair and their soul eaten by the industry.

During the summer I spent editing this work, I helped my five-year-old son start his first pony. The boy named the pony Fred. My son was fairly shy about the whole process and a bit scared when it came to riding, but in the evenings, when he had finished his chores, my son would slip down to Fred's stall and sit with him while Ol' Fred ate his supper. The boy spoke with Fred about many things and showed him his LEGOs or his new shoes, and he whispered secrets to Fred with confidence that the secrets were safe. They are. Ponies are good secret keepers, and horses are too. As a professional, I tend to forget the things that truly start us on the road to horsemanship, the things that are warm and spontaneous. Most evenings I find myself drifting down to the barn, rye whiskey in hand, unconscious of what I am doing. I make the excuse that I am there to have one last look at my wards before dark. I look at their legs and listen to their breathing, and in rusty light I am blanketed with the sounds of happy horses eating good hay, shifting here and there, slapping their lips in the water buckets, sneezing, sighing, and groaning. Somewhere under those sounds are the words I wish I could write about horses. I think the words are about dancing the silence down through the morning, but that is not my work. That is the work of Adam Duritz and others. The words may be the question of who is the boxer and who is the bag, but "Yellow Ledbetter" is Eddie Vedder's work, and "Mexico City Blues" belongs to Kerouac. So I am left with Bukowski's advice, and I don't try.

I am drawn toward horses, and I seek to make the voiceless movement of their limbs my own voice. I cannot sing well enough that anyone would care to hear. I cannot dance well enough that anyone would care to watch. I cannot play an instrument nor paint nor shape marble into an everlasting monument, but I can ride, and when I ride, if I am careful and mindful I can express myself to the world.

THE NEXT THREE YEARS

Some years ago, I was at a Christmas party. Everyone there was a horseman in some regard because we humans tend to seek out those that are most like us. I got to talking to a farrier that allowed that he started a few colts a year for the public. At that time, I ran several crews that started horses for several large horse operations around the country. Between myself and the crew, we started an average of three hundred plus horses a year, plus weaning and halter breaking that many more and also altering a large number of colts into geldings. At the peak, I personally put the first ride on 360-some odd horses in one year. Because my name was on the contract, I felt responsible for putting at least the first ride on everything. This was mercenary work, and while I learned a lot and did the best work I could, I feel a little ashamed about the "factory" starting methods that I used to get the contracts done on schedule. Nevertheless, that was the way of things, and upon hearing this, the farrier was taken aback. He said, "Man, you must really love starting colts." It was my turn to be taken aback. I had never thought about whether I liked to start colts or not. I just did it. I replied, "Not so much, I really love finishing horses, but someone has to start the colts first."

For the record, I do like starting colts. That's handy for me because I spend the majority of my time doing it, but truly, as much as I like to start colts, I really like finishing horses; and before a horse can be finished, a significant amount of training between the start and the finish must be done. As a general rule, this training takes about three years, no matter the horse or the discipline. There are futurity trainers in the world that can get an amazing amount of work done on a horse in just a year, but the honest ones will tell you that the futurity winner is still a long way from being finished. As important as the start of a young horse is, the years of training that follow are every bit as important and must be regarded as such.

In recent years, a lot of attention has been focused on starting colts. Untold amounts of money have been spent on videos and clinics. Mine is yet one of hundreds of books written on the subject. Competitions are even being held to find out who can do the best job fastest. (I find this disgusting.) However, not that much time and energy is being spent on discussing and teaching the next three years of advanced training that goes into a fine-finished horse. My original intention was to write this book about training a horse and preparing the horse for the finishing process, but I found that I could not discuss training until I properly discussed starting. I wrote *A Started Colt* so I could write this book, *The Next Three Years*.

THE WALK

The walk is the training gait. Through the walk, we advance the horse and balance the horse, we warm the horse up in a walk, and we cool the horse down in the walk. We introduce all new maneuvers in the walk, and we further refine all known maneuvers in the walk. We cannot train until we can walk. The walk is a four-beat gait in which all four feet lift and fall independently. The independence of the feet is the key to the walk because, through independence, we gain balance and rhythm.

I spend a lot of time advancing the walking gait of a horse in training. I didn't always. I was in too much of a hurry, but anymore the first thirty days of training are dedicated almost entirely to the walk, and a good portion of time in the years to come are spent extending and collecting the horse at a walk in an effort to build fitness in the muscles for extension and collection in the other gaits. In a balanced and rhythmic walk, we are able to slowly frame the horse into a collected gait where the majority of the horse's weight and the center of balance are shifted back onto the hindquarters. In so doing, we not only build supple fitness in the structure but also rehabilitate past injuries or strains that the horse inevitably suffered in the starting process and before.

Training the Walk and Training at the Walk

In order to train at the walk, we must first train the horse to walk. Of course, the horse was compelled to walk as well as trot and probably lope while being started, but a true extended walk—with independent extension from all four limbs, a lifted back, a loose, framed neck—that is the start of self-carriage and impulsion starting from the hind legs takes actual step-by-step training.

About the Author

Bret Davis is a native of Southern Oregon and grew up in the west coast stock horse culture of the area. In his late teens he commenced a career of traveling around the country and the world working for large horse and cattle operations. From race horses to Dressage to Cutting horses and working ranch horses in both North and South America, Bret has learned that Horsemanship is an art to be practiced but it can never truly be perfected.

Bret now resides in Northern Arizona and oversees the colt starting operation for one of the states largest ranches. Each year Bret halter breaks and starts upward of fifty colts a year to be used on the ranch and later go on to have performance careers. With each young horse that passes under his care he learns more about his craft and his canvas.